P9-CPY-347

FRANCHISING IN CANADA

FRANCHISING IN CANADA
Pros and Cons

Michael M. Coltman

International Self-Counsel Press Ltd.
Head and Editorial Office
Vancouver
Toronto   Seattle

Copyright © 1982 by International Self-Counsel Press Ltd.
All rights reserved.
No part of this book may be reproduced or transmitted in any form by
any means without permission in writing from the publisher, except by a
reviewer, who may quote brief passages in a review.
Printed in Canada

First edition: January, 1982; Reprinted: June, 1985
Second edition: July, 1987

Canadian Cataloguing in Publication Data

Coltman, Michael M. (Michael Macdonald), 1930-
    Franchising in Canada

    (Self-Counsel series)
    ISBN 0-88908-667-2

    1. Franchises (Retail trade) — Canada.
I. Title.   II. Series.
HF5429.235.C2C64 1987 658.8'7'00971 C87-091300-X

International Self-Counsel Press Ltd.
Head and Editorial Office
1481 Charlotte Road
North Vancouver, British Columbia V7J 1H1
Vancouver   Toronto   Seattle

CONTENTS

PREFACE

It's Saturday and you have a busy slate of tasks ahead of you. To start the day, it's a breakfast at McDonald's, followed by a visit to Beaver Lumber for some hardware, a stop at Canadian Tire for some auto accessories and then an appointment at H & R Block to complete your income tax return, followed by a stop at Goliger's to pick up the air ticket for next week's business trip and a stop at Shoppers Drug Mart for some toiletries. Since it's almost lunchtime, a visit to the local A & W (next door to the Holiday Inn) for a hamburger will provide sustenance for the afternoon's shopping: U-Frame-It for a picture that needs framing, Busy Bee to pick up some dry cleaning, Midas Muffler to check an exhaust problem, Grandma Lee's to purchase some bakery goods, and finally home to your house recently purchased with the help of Century 21.

There seems nothing unusual about this day's activities, but in fact there is. Each of the places visited, including the return to the family residence, mentions the name of a franchised company.

Today, it appears that everywhere you look new enterprises are opening up that offer some form of good or service that is supported by a franchise form of business, whether it be a fast food restaurant (and some not so fast food), a leisure and travel business, a retail clothing store, a real estate company, or a company specializing in tax returns.

There are an estimated 650 to 700 franchising organizations operating in Canada, of which about two-thirds are Canadian and the rest, for the most part, American. However, these franchise organizations comprise approximately 25 000 independent, individual franchise entrepreneurs operating their own franchise outlets, while about 5 000 other franchises are owned by franchisors. Franchised companies operate in all provinces, but the majority are located in British Columbia and Ontario.

Many Canadians have already learned of the benefits and opportunities of this rapidly growing form of business. If you have been thinking about getting into some form of franchise business, this book may well be able to help you.

However, do not be attracted by the bait of quick profits for minimum effort, low initial investment, and freedom to be your own boss. There are still too many entrepreneurs who, in evaluating a franchise, disregard warning lights, push aside sensible (generally negative) advice, and fail to completely examine the franchisor or the contract, even when the franchisor suggests that this be done.

Some franchisees end up being very well off, but by far the majority find themselves working harder than they anticipated under contractual arrangements that may seem harsh or restrictive since they do not provide the anticipated return on investment. Some of these entrepreneurs fail; they expected too much from too little effort on their part.

This book is written primarily for the entrepreneur who wishes to start his or her own business. However, an initial word of caution: as a franchised business operator do not mislead yourself into thinking you have complete independence. A franchisee has a degree of independence, but, as you will find out, is controlled to a greater or lesser degree (depending on the type of franchise) by the franchisor.

On the other hand, with success and with growth, it may well be that the individual who runs a successful franchised business will eventually become a franchisor, selling franchises to others who wish to become franchisees.

Note: At the back of this book is a worksheet to use which will help you organize the information you need to have before making a decision about investing in a franchise.

1

FRANCHISING: AN INTRODUCTION

Franchising as a means for independent entrepreneurs to go into business for themselves has been booming for the last 20 years, and there appears to be no immediate let up in sight. You only need to look at popular business journals and newspaper business sections, or even in the business opportunities section of newspaper classified advertising, to see the many references made to franchised businesses.

Franchising is simply a form of distribution of a good or a service. Because of its high profile in the fast food industry, franchising has often been identified primarily with that type of business. But, as you will know from reading the preface to this book, we all use many other types of franchise goods or services each day of our lives without perhaps even realizing it.

a. A DEFINITION OF FRANCHISING

There is no commonly accepted definition of franchising that can be applied in all cases. However, in general terms, it is a method of distribution or marketing in which a company (the franchisor) grants by contract to an individual or another company (the franchisee) the right to carry on a business in a prescribed way in a particular location for a specified period.

The franchisee may be allowed to operate only one establishment or may be given an area in which a number of franchised outlets may be operated. That area could be a city, a province, a major portion of the country, or indeed the whole country. For example, a few years ago, Wendy's in the U.S. gave a private Canadian company the territorial rights to all of Canada for Wendy's restaurant operations.

1

1. Fees

For the services that it provides, the franchisor receives a fee, or royalty, usually based on gross sales, or else a fixed fee (for example, a flat monthly or annual amount, or a fixed fee based on the number of rooms in a hotel or motel franchise).

In addition, the franchisee usually has to pay a share of local, regional, or national advertising costs. Again, this advertising cost is usually a percentage of sales revenue. The fees and other costs are generally payable monthly.

For what you pay as a franchisee, you may receive business advice and counsel, financial aid (direct or indirect), market research, lease negotiation, site evaluation, building plans, training programs, national advertising, an accounting system, and an established and widely recognized name and image.

Although you must provide, or arrange for, most of the financing required, the franchisor may provide some of this initial capital. In such cases, the monthly fee will probably include an extra amount to pay back this franchisor financing, with interest. However, even if you have to arrange for the entire financing yourself, the franchisor's credit strength and reputation can be of help in seeking a loan. Later chapters cover financing and how to go about seeking loans.

2. Requirements

As a franchisee, you will be required to maintain certain standards established by the franchisor. As an individual franchisee you may see these standards (such as pricing policies, or the requirement to purchase products from the franchisor at a higher price than you can buy them locally) as an imposition on you as an independent entrepreneur. But, on the other hand, you have to consider the benefits of increased business that national advertising can produce. As an individual operator, you could never afford that kind of advertising coverage.

b. A BRIEF HISTORY OF FRANCHISING

Although it is thought that some forms of franchising occurred in Europe in the 18th century, this did not have any great impact on the way most business was conducted. In fact, franchising's major impact began in the U.S. when the Singer Sewing Machine Company initiated a manufacturer/retailer distribution franchise system following the Civil War.

At the turn of the 19th century, the industrial revolution gained momentum in the U.S., and the resulting advances in technology combined with a good transportation system and improved communication set the stage for mass production and distribution. Manufacturers and producers quickly realized that the distribution of their products to the marketplace was a key element in their success as producers.

The automobile industry grew rapidly as the manufacturers established a relationship with franchised dealers (retailers). Similarly, soft drink producers realized they would have problems shipping bottled soft drinks over great distances and therefore established local franchise producers operating under licence. A third major force that began franchising in this period was the petroleum industry, which moved its products to the market through independent dealers.

1. Boom period

The period after World War II saw a tremendous surge in the acceptance of the franchising concept. This period, through to about the mid 60s, is often called the boom period of franchising. The boom is generally attributed to the mobility of the North American public and its heavy reliance on services. During this period, many new categories of franchising were developed, such as fast food restaurants, cleaning establishments, equipment rental stores, automobile and trailer rentals, motels, recreation services, and accounting and other business services. The

3

franchisor companies' shares on the stock markets became the glamour stocks of this era and, at the time, the sky seemed to be the limit to the franchising phenomenon.

Unfortunately, the stock market boom in these glamour stocks began to fall apart, primarily because of adverse publicity over a number of the franchise schemes in the fast food industry built around famous personalities. Because of these "names," the franchisors were able to charge exorbitantly high initial fees to franchisees, while providing little in return in the way of operating services or training. This, combined with what seemed like high interest rates at that time (they would be considered low today), caused the failure of many franchisors. One of the more famous (or infamous) was that of Minnie Pearl (a chicken franchise scheme). By the summer of 1969, close to 2 000 franchises had been sold in North America, but less than 200 actually opened, and none of these survived.

Such abuses, and, in some cases, illegal practices, resulted in court decisions and restrictive regulations (primarily in the U.S.) that created a slow down in franchise expansion, particularly in the fast food restaurant category.

2. Solid base develops

However, this retrenchment was finally overcome. Over the past 20 years, the franchising method of distribution of goods and services has built a solid base and expanded into many new areas, such as auto products, income tax services, cosmetics, and even real estate. Franchising has matured. Its growth rate is steady, and once again many established companies see it as an attractive way to expand. For example, not all franchise companies start out as franchisors. Companies that already have a successful operation in their own right can decide to go into franchising as Beaver Lumber Company did a few years ago when Beaver believed that their new rural outlets could prosper best by being franchised to individuals who invested in them. Franchisors with little to offer are being eliminated; the ones that remain will be those with experience and management competence.

4

c. ADVANTAGES OF FRANCHISING TO THE INDIVIDUAL FRANCHISEE

Some of the major advantages for the individual franchisee of taking the franchise route into business are discussed below.

It is possible to start up as a generally independent entrepreneur but with the support of an established parent company, the franchisor. The franchisor may provide you with possible assistance in such matters as obtaining financing, site selection, building construction supervision, employee training, and support during the difficult break-in period subsequent to opening.

As a franchisee, you have the opportunity to buy into an established concept, although this, by itself, is no guarantee that you will succeed. However, the risk of failure is generally reduced. Statistics show that the independent entrepreneur opening a small business stands a 70 to 80% chance of *not* surviving the first few critical years. Similar statistics show there is an 80% chance of *success* for a franchisee.

You have the ongoing assistance and problem-solving ability of the franchisor, who can afford to hire specialists in the head office in such areas as cost control, marketing and sales, and research and development.

The franchisor can provide local, regional, or even national advertising (albeit at a cost to you).

You have access to credit that you may not otherwise have. Chartered banks and similar lending institutions are usually more willing to lend money to an entrepreneur who has the backing of a successful franchisor than they are to the completely independent entrepreneur.

You may be able to purchase supplies at a reduced cost since the franchisor can purchase in bulk and pass the savings on to the franchisees. (As much as 3 to 6% may be saved on costs this way.)

You may find an opportunity to take over a turnkey franchise operation. A turnkey operation is one where the franchisor provides you with a completely set up franchise and does the following for you:

(a) Assists in obtaining financing

5

(b) Evaluates, selects, and acquires a site

(c) Constructs and equips the premises

(d) Trains you and your staff

(e) Purchases the initial inventory

(f) Provides management and accounting reporting systems

(g) Provides advertising, public relations and marketing services

(h) After opening, provides ongoing supervision and guidance

In other words, about all you have to do is turn the key in the door and you're in business.

You may also have an advantage if you buy a franchise already tested in the U.S. You will have the protection of a system already developed, with the bugs taken out. The time lag between what happens in the U.S. and in Canada is about five years, and in that period a lot of start up problems can be solved.

Finally, franchising offers many of the advantages of an integrated chain business (without some of the disadvantages) because of the voluntary nature of the contract rather than central ownership.

d. DISADVANTAGES OF FRANCHISING TO THE INDIVIDUAL FRANCHISEE

Just as you must consider the advantages of the franchised form of business, you must also consider the following disadvantages.

The cost of the services provided by the franchisor comes off the top of your sales revenue and could add up to 10% or more of that revenue.

Even though the franchise arrangement allows you to start a business that you might otherwise only be able to begin with difficulty, you will have some loss of freedom since the franchisor's standards have to be adhered to, and you may have limited scope for individual personal initiative.

In some cases, the markup that the franchisor adds to the products that you must buy from him or her can increase your operating costs, particularly if an equally good product could be purchased locally at a lower cost.

Experience shows that you run some risk of not achieving the sales potential, and thus the profit, that the franchisor stated was possible when selling the franchise.

If the franchisor operates from a jurisdiction other than the one in which you have the franchise and does not fulfill his or her obligations, it can be difficult, if not impossible, to seek redress.

e. LEGAL ASPECTS OF FRANCHISING

If you purchase a franchise in Canada, it will likely be one that was developed either in the U.S. or in this country. About two-thirds of the franchisors operating in this country are Canadian and, indeed, a number of Canadian-developed franchises have moved successfully into the U.S. (Keg restaurants and Shoppers Drug Mart, for example).

Although many states have laws and regulations governing franchise companies, the same is not true of Canada. Currently, Alberta is the only province with specific legislation covering franchising. However, Quebec has extended its Securities Act to cover franchising.

In all other situations franchise relationships are governed by general federal laws such as the Combines Investigation Act (which deals with competition and trade practice matters) and the Trade Marks Act (dealing with registration and protection of trade marks). There are also provincial laws, such as those that cover business or trade practices, corporate statutes, and consumer protection. These vary from province to province and usually apply more to the franchisee-consumer relationship than to the franchisee-franchisor.

As franchising grows, it is possible that franchise legislation will be enacted in other provinces.

The Alberta Act imposes restrictions on franchisors operating in that province. The act's regulations require disclosure of the material facts involved in operating the franchise. This requires that a prospectus be filed with the Securities Commission. The prospectus outlines the franchisor's financial capabilities and the history of the franchise company and of its principals. This information can be useful in assessing the stability of the franchise.

As a prospective franchisee in Alberta, you would be entitled to a copy of the prospectus, which can be quite revealing. One filed with the Alberta Securities Commission includes the following paragraph: "There is no assurance that the franchisee will ever make a profit, nor is there any assurance that municipal, provincial or federal requirements which the franchisee may have to comply with, will be met or licences, if any, granted."

Of course, a franchisor would be very unwise in a prospectus to guarantee the franchisee a profit, but if you read the above paragraph as a prospective franchisee, you might well wonder what you were getting into!

A franchisor operating in other provinces in Canada does not have to file a prospectus with the provincial government. So, for the most part, as a franchisee, you are on your own, although in British Columbia, the Trade Practices Act does have a provision that protects the first time franchisee. The provision reads as follows: "If a person goes into a business opportunity scheme where he has to spend money and also work himself, and has no experience in that type of business, he is considered to be a consumer for the purpose of the statute."

Ideally it would be best if there were a uniform set of franchisor and franchisee standards across the country, but that seems unlikely to happen soon since most provinces are not showing much interest in adopting disclosure regulations (such as Alberta's) and it may be a number of years before we catch up in this area with the U.S. In the U.S., the tendency is to view the franchisee as a consumer who has the right to protection against unethical franchisors. The tendency in Canada is to view the franchisee as a businessperson dealing with another businessperson on an equal basis.

A recent court decision tends to bear out this point. The franchisee was suing the franchisor for alleged misrepresentation by the franchisor who made oral statements that misled the franchisee about the profitability of the business. The court ruled in favor of the franchisor because the contract itself stated that oral representations were not part of the contract. The court also ruled that the franchisee was an experienced businessperson who had received professional advice before the contract was signed. This latter point might imply that, had the franchisee been inexperienced in business and not received professional advice, he or she might have had some protection, such as that offered by the B.C. Trade Practices Act mentioned earlier.

However, regardless of the situation, one of your best friends, if you are contemplating a franchise purchase, will be a lawyer. Choose one who is up to date on the legal aspects of franchising. Even a reputable franchisor may have overlooked something that your lawyer (who is aware of all the local and provincial laws such as building codes and health regulations) might notice in the contract that should be changed. The topic of franchise contracts will be covered in a later chapter.

f. U.S. BASED FRANCHISOR

U.S. based franchisors have two ways of operating in Canada. They can operate entirely from the U.S. without any company-owned offices in this country. This would mean that all servicing of the franchisee (a critical aspect for the franchisee's success) will be done from the U.S. head office which may, or may not, be close to the Canadian border.

The other way they can operate is to grant an area franchise to the Canadian franchisor (which Wendy's restaurants has done), with the Canadian company then responsible for the site selection, training, advertising, and other aspects of a successful franchisor/franchisee arrangement.

Regardless of the method used, the franchisor would have to file a prospectus if operating in Alberta (a franchisee is allowed four days after receipt of the required disclosure to repudiate the franchise contract under the Alberta legislation).

If the franchisor is operating from a U.S. base, you should be able to obtain a copy of the prospectus from the Securities Commission of the state in which it is filed (and most states now require the franchisor to register this kind of disclosure).

g. IN SUMMARY

Despite its disadvantages, a franchised business generally offers real advantages with, perhaps, considerably reduced risks over going it on your own. Remember, however, that franchising can not guarantee a profit. You, as the business operator, are ultimately responsible for the success or failure of the venture. This is probably the most important sentence in this book so let me repeat it: you are ultimately responsible for the success or failure of the venture.

2
TYPES OF FRANCHISES

The traditional types of franchising (automobile and truck dealers, petroleum service stations, and soft drink bottlers) have been a dominant force in the franchise field and, despite some decline in this type of franchise outlet, still account for about 75% of total franchise sales revenue.

However, there are many other types of what are referred to as business format franchises that can offer you opportunities for going into business for yourself. Let us have a look at some of them.

a. RETAILING
Retailing has long been the giant in the business format franchise field. In particular, the fast food restaurant business, which accounts for about one-third of all business format franchising, has predominated.

1. Fast food
A fast food operation is usually distinctive and easily recognizable. Frequently, it has a limited menu as well as take-out service. This type of fast food operation is still a leader in the field, although some types of sit down restaurants are moving into this area.

Many of the entrepreneurs who obtained franchises in the early days of fast food franchising were able to control a particular territory and prospered along with the franchisor. Indeed, in some cases the multiownership of franchises has resulted in chains within chains, with some franchisees actually now larger in dollar strength than their franchisors. Despite this, many opportunities still exist for prospective franchisors with new, small, expanding chains that can offer a good product to franchisees.

11

The fast food field runs the whole gamut from hamburgers, hot dogs, french fries, and milkshakes, to pizza, barbecued beef or ribs, fried chicken, steaks, Mexican food, seafood, pancakes and waffles, roast beef sandwiches, and fast food pies to name only a few.

2. Convenience food stores

Convenience food stores (such as Mac's) have grown substantially in both number of outlets and dollar volume. Convenience stores offer consumers the many everyday fill-in items that they need between regular visits to the larger supermarkets.

Convenience stores, over the years, have been adept at introducing innovative operating techniques such as offering take-out sandwiches, or hot food items precooked by the supplier and needing only reheating (for example, in a microwave oven) for consumption. Growing numbers of convenience stores are associated with gasoline stations.

3. Food retailing other than convenience stores

Food retailing by food stores other than convenience stores is seen in specialty or health food shops, donut shops, ice cream parlors, coffee service outlets, bakeries, and candy stores. In particular, ice cream stores have gained in popularity and expanded rapidly in the past few years.

4. Product retailing

Product retailing covers a wide range of products from general merchandise to clothing or other wearing apparel, catalogue sales, cosmetics, drugs, electronics, home furnishings, fashion fabrics, paint and wallpaper, building supplies, records, hardware, mattresses, gift stores, gourmet kitchenware, light fixtures, luggage, picture framing, and photofinishing to name only a few. New types of franchise retail stores are continually popping up.

5. Auto products and services

In the area of auto products and services, retail outlets of tire manufacturers lead the field. In addition, these outlets often sell a full range of auto services, such as rust protection, mufflers, auto waxing, car accessories, brake parts, and, frequently, significant amounts of non-automotive products such as radios and television sets, other household appliances, garden supplies, and similar products.

Other franchises in this category would include car wash companies, parking services, and diagnostic shops.

b. LEISURE AND TRAVEL

In the past decade or so the trend toward a shorter work week, longer vacations, an increased number of statutory holidays, increasing disposable income, and earlier retirement have all contributed to the growth of leisure and travel business format franchises.

Included in this category would be travel agents, sun tan parlors, and other recreation, entertainment, and travel businesses.

Hotels, motels, and campgrounds would also fit in this category. The hotel and motel franchising segment has shown solid growth (despite the mounting costs of energy) over the last decade. The computerization of both national and international reservation systems has contributed to this growth.

One new element that has emerged is referred to as the budget motel; it offers a minimum of frills and a very low room rate. Franchised campgrounds have also appeared during this period.

c. BUSINESS AND PERSONAL SERVICES

Because of the growing complexities of the business world today there appears to be a growing demand for many diverse business and personal service companies that can provide opportunities for franchisees.

1. Leasing and rental services

In the area of leasing and rental services, the largest category is the passenger car (including used car) and truck rental business. In addition, there appears to be an increasing trend toward outlets renting other kinds of equipment, such as gardening supplies, tools, medical equipment, party supplies, and video cassette movies.

2. Business aids and services

In the category of business aids and services are many varied and specialized franchises, including accounting, employment services, general business systems, printing and copying, tax return preparation, and many similar types of business.

Also included in this category would be suppliers of background music, engineering and marketing consultants, security system businesses, and, a relatively recent entrant, franchised real estate companies.

3. Personal services

The personal service category includes those franchises that offer home construction, improvement, or cleaning and maintenance services. In particular, the growth in on-location carpet and upholstery cleaning in homes (as well as offices, institutions, and plants) is apparent. Indeed, some franchise companies include cleaning walls, and fixtures, along with floor services. This cleaning service might include such things as mothproofing, soil and flame retarding treatment, minor carpet repairs, and carpet static removal.

Outdoor services offer lawn and garden care, including automated lawn care and lawn problem analysis. Franchise companies also specialize in the sale, construction, and maintenance of swimming pools.

Other companies in this category include those offering water conditioning, burglar and fire alarm systems, construction and renovation of floors and walls, cabinets and paneling, and even outdoor pavement and driveway maintenance.

4. Educational services

In the area of educational services, there has been a growth of franchisors offering dietary and exercise training, as well as secretarial and/or computer training.

14

d. LOOKING TO THE FUTURE

1. The general point of view

What of the future? What types of franchise establishments are expected to be those more favored in the next few years? The following might be the best ones to look at:

(a) Business and personal service companies, such as real estate, employment agencies, printing and copying, paper shredding, record storage, and office layout.

(b) Fast food establishments are also expected to continue to predominate, but their menus may include more health food items and foods for calorie conscious diners. Theme and/or ethnic food restaurants will be popular.

(c) Franchises related to the travel and leisure business may also grow, and public interest in health and fitness may create a demand for more dance clubs, fitness and health clubs, and sporting goods stores to fill the need for recreational items.

(d) Professionals are also starting to franchise and you will probably see the emergence of franchised accounting offices, legal clinics, and medical and dental facilities. In fact, perhaps more likely in the U.S. initially (where banking regulations are less restrictive) banks may begin to franchise, with small town banks becoming part of a large franchised banking system.

(e) Home entertainment will also be at the forefront, with stores offering home computers, electronic games, videocassettes, videodisks and compact disk players.

(f) Auto care has always been strong in franchising, but newer types of business might emerge. For example, one company is now offering to color coordinate your tires with your car. Some industry observers suggest you may see the strong development of one-stop car care facilities, with several operations under one roof much like shopping centres (such as convenience food stores) with franchised restaurants around the perimeter of a central seating area.

(g) Firms specializing in franchisee financing, accounting, and consulting may also appear in more numbers.

Industrial franchising is another new trend that is increasing in popularity. While it does not have as high a profile as those franchise companies in the retail or mass consumer markets, the concept is the same. It includes truck wash and lubrication services, commercial burglar and theft alarms, piped-in music, machine vending, and similar concepts that appeal to the wholesale, rather than the retail, market.

One other emerging trend in franchisor/franchisee relationships is the establishment of franchisee associations or councils. These councils are initially organized by franchisors but are made up primarily, if not entirely, of franchisees with a common interest in a particular franchise system. The associations deal with a wide range of problems, but their major interest is in the direction and expenditure of the advertising budgets, the contribution to franchisor decisions and plans, and the melding of the interests of both franchisor and franchisees.

2. The government's point of view

And what is the government's view of the future of franchising? The following major trends and developments were anticipated by the federal Department of Regional Industrial Expansion (DRIE):

(a) Franchising will continue to grow at a rapid rate in Canada.

(b) Franchising will become a major factor in more types of business activity in Canada.

(c) More Canadian firms, and especially those with an existing strong local base, will begin to use franchising to expand regionally, nationally, and internationally, especially into the U.S.

(d) Major corporations will continue to purchase successful franchise systems; in particular, the large food processors will add to their already major ownership portfolio of fast food franchise systems.

(e) Additional U.S. franchise systems will enter the Canadian market. The large number of U.S. controlled franchise systems already in Canada will continue to expand rapidly.

(f) Additional European franchise systems, mainly French and British, will enter the Canadian market. These franchise systems will import inventory from Europe on a substantial, continuing basis similar to what is now occurring with existing French systems in Canada.

(g) Additional Japanese franchise systems may enter Canada as a direct result of the rapid development of franchising in Japan.

3

GETTING STARTED

a. ARE YOU SUITED TO RUNNING A BUSINESS?

Before you embark on a business venture of your own it might be a good idea to try the following self-test of 10 simple questions. After each question check the answer that describes how you feel, or comes closest to it. It is important to be honest with yourself.

SELF-TEST

1. How do you react to other people?
   - (a) I like people and get along with almost everybody.
   - (b) I have lots of friends and don't need any more.
   - (c) Other people bug me.

2. Are you a self-motivator?
   - (a) I start things myself, and I don't need others to get me motivated.
   - (b) Sometimes I need others to get me going.
   - (c) Why should I put myself out until I have to?

3. What about leadership potential?
   - (a) When I begin something most people seem to go along with it.
   - (b) I'm all right as long as someone gives me some direction.
   - (c) Once someone gets things going, I'll cooperate as long as I agree with it.

4. Are you a good organizer?
   - (a) I like to plan ahead; even if someone comes up with a

good idea, I'm usually the one to map out the plan.

(b) Planning isn't that necessary; as long as things work out I feel O.K.

(c) What's the point in planning? Someone will just come along and screw it up.

5. Can you handle responsibility?

(a) I'm a take charge person. Someone has to take control and see things through.

(b) If nobody else will take charge, I don't mind accepting the responsibility.

(c) Why should I bother when I can leave it to those who want to show how smart they are at assuming control?

6. Do you like work?

(a) If it's something I want, I'll work as long and as hard as necessary.

(b) I find I can only work so much at a task before bowing out.

(c) Hard work is for fools.

7. What about perseverance?

(a) Nothing stops me once I've decided a goal is worthwhile.

(b) As long as it doesn't get screwed up by someone else, I'll finish what I start.

(c) If I see things might not work out I quit. Why fight a losing battle?

8. Are you able to make decisions?

(a) I can make decisions, and more than 50% of the time I'm correct.

(b) I need time to make decisions. I have to talk to everybody involved. Most of the time they give me wrong advice.

(c) Why should I always have to make decisions that are other people's responsibility?

9. Are you determined?
   (a) Once I have decided to go ahead with a project nothing gets in my way.
   (b) As long as someone else doesn't get in my way I can usually finish what I start.
   (c) If things go right from the beginning, I'll persevere until there is a problem.

10. What about your health?
   (a) I'm full of energy seven days a week.
   (b) I'm full of energy for the things I like to do.
   (c) How come all my friends and acquaintances are so full of energy?

Now count up the score:
   (a) Number of check marks beside the first answer to each question: _____
   (b) Number of check marks beside the second answer to each question: _____
   (c) Number of check marks beside the third answer to each question: _____

If most of your check marks are beside the first answers, you probably have the right qualities to run your own business. If not, your chances of success are considerably lessened, and you might find it a good idea to work with a partner who is stronger in the areas where you have a weakness. If most of your checks are alongside the third answer, not even a great partner will be able to prop you up.

b. FRANCHISE SYSTEM COSTS

What kind of costs are involved for the franchisee to get into business? This question is an impossible one to answer. It depends entirely on the type of franchise that one is looking at.

The start-up cash required may be as low as a few thousand dollars in some service business franchises (such as, for example, a collection agency) or for a dealership or distributorship type of franchise to as much as several million dollars for an entire hotel or motel franchise where you would have to own both land and building.

The only rule of thumb is that you will probably pay more for a strong, healthy franchise than for a comparable one from a franchisor with a new product on the market.

c. LEGAL FORMS OF ORGANIZATION

Once you have decided to go into business, one of the earliest decisions that needs to be made is the organizational form, from a legal point of view, that the enterprise will take. The three common types of organization are the proprietorship, the partnership, and the incorporated company or corporation.

1. Proprietorship

The easiest way for an owner/operator to establish a firm with little or no cost or legal problems is to form a sole proprietorship. Many businesses are operated this way, with the owner responsible for the actions and liabilities of the business, even if the day-to-day running of it, or parts of it, is delegated to others.

Proprietorships are usually financed primarily from the owner's personal savings, from bank loans, sometimes from government loans, and, if it is successful, from the net income of the business reinvested in it.

The net income of the proprietorship is the personal income of the owner and is taxed, with any salary paid by the business, at personal tax rates. Any loans from creditors or investors are made to the owner, not the company.

Proprietorships do not issue shares of any kind, as do incorporated companies (which will be discussed later). Businesses established as proprietorships are still subject to regulatory authorities.

The main advantages of establishing a proprietorship are that the owner has total control (although in a franchised company some of this control can be eroded by controls imposed by the franchisor), does not have to consider the opinions of partners or other business

21

associates (thus speeding the decision-making process), and will reap the full financial rewards.

Some disadvantages are that, theoretically, the company ceases to exist when the owner dies and the assets of the company become part of the owner's estate and are subject to estate and inheritance taxes. Thus it may be difficult to continue the business.

A proprietorship may also find it difficult to expand since it does not have the same opportunities to raise capital as do other types of business organizations that have a broader base of financial resources (although, in a franchised business, the franchisor may be of considerable help in this regard).

Also, generally speaking, in case of bankruptcy, the proprietor's personal assets as well as the company's assets may be seized to satisfy the liabilities of the proprietorship. In other words, the proprietor's liability is unlimited.

2. Partnership

Unlike the sole proprietorship, the partnership is generally a more formal type of business organization. It is a legal association between two or more individuals or co-owners of a business. Although a partnership does not require a written agreement, all partners probably should agree to a negotiated contract, or articles of partnership. The terms of these articles will vary widely from one enterprise to another, but they should include at least the name of the company; the name of each partner; the rights, contributions, and benefits of each partner; and the length of the life of the partnership. The two most common types of partnership are the general and the limited.

In a general partnership, each partner may represent the company and enter into contracts on its behalf. Each partner is also personally liable for the debts of the company incurred by other partners. This personal liability (as is also the case in a sole proprietorship) is unlimited.

A limited partnership, on the other hand, has both general partners with unlimited personal liability and limited partners with limited personal liability. The partnership contract should spell out this limited personal liability. It should also indicate the amount that the limited partner(s) have invested.

A limited partnership arrangement is made when limited, or silent, partners wish to invest in a company and obtain a return on their investment without being personally involved in the day-to-day decision making and operation of the business.

General and limited partnerships are not taxed at the incorporated company tax rates. Instead, the company's net income, or loss, is shared according to the terms of the partnership contract, and each partner includes that share, plus any salary received from the company, on his or her personal tax return.

Partnerships, like proprietorships, do not issue shares of any kind, and must conform to regulatory authorities.

The advantages of partnerships are that financing is frequently easier to obtain and, since there is more than one owner, the total partnership investment can be much greater than it can in a proprietorship. A partnership may also have a greater depth of combined judgment and managerial skills.

Disadvantages are that upon one partner's death or withdrawal from the business, the partnership may have to be dissolved and reorganized. This can make it difficult to continue the company's operations. It can also create financial difficulties for the company if the dead partner's heirs disagree with the company's evaluation of the deceased's share of the company.

Also, the heirs will have to be bought out, which may impose a financial burden on the remaining partners. Another disadvantage of the partnership is that, since in many cases all partners may need to be consulted, quick decisions about the company's operations may be difficult to make. Finally, it may be difficult to remove an incompetent partner. The business partners you select should thus be chosen with care.

3. Corporation
The majority of businesses are probably organized as incorporated companies or corporations. The corporation,

unlike the proprietorship and partnership, is a separate legal entity, with its own rights and duties, that can continue as a separate business even after the death of an owner.

Establishing a corporation is both more complex and more costly than establishing a proprietorship or a partnership but, despite these problems, is probably the most effective way of operating a company.

Companies may be established as either public or private. A public company is generally one that has its shares listed on a stock exchange. Some of the franchisors that you are in contact with may well be public companies. The legal requirements for operating a public company are much more strict than those for a private company. Therefore, as a franchisee, you will more likely be interested in organizing a private company since that type of company is designed for the operator of a small business.

Companies can be incorporated in a single province, in one or more provinces, or federally. Since you will probably start out by operating your franchise in a single location, you need to incorporate only in that province. You can have a lawyer do this for you or, in many cases, you can do this for yourself since books are available that show you step by step how this is done. Doing it yourself may save you several hundred dollars. However, if the situation, for one reason or another, is complex, then professional legal advice should be sought. For example, depending on your personal financial situation, there may be advantages to establishing the share structure of the company one way rather than another.

The major advantage of the corporate form of business is that, generally speaking, since the company is a separate legal entity, the individual owners cannot be held responsible for the company's liabilities. The owners, in other words, have a liability limited to their investment in the company. However, despite this, lending institutions that you approach for financing will generally make you sign a personal note to extend your liability outside the protection offered by the company.

Another advantage is that financing may be facilitated by the creation of easily transferable certificates of ownership, known as shares, that may be bought by or sold to others, including employees of the company. (Note, however, that most provinces have restrictions concerning the ownership of shares in private corporations.) This broadens the base of financing available to the company. The limited liability of share ownership appeals to some investors since it permits ownership, with a potential return on the investment, without involvement in the company's day-to-day operations.

There may also be some personal tax advantages to forming a limited company (such as being able to use the lower corporate rate of tax) that make the corporate form of business appealing. Since each individual situation is different you should consult your accountant for the tax pros and cons of forming an incorporated company.

For regulatory purposes, a corporation is like a person. It can sue and be sued, just like an individual, and it must conform to regulatory authorities. A corporation is an ongoing organization with an infinite life of its own even though employees and owners come and go. Many of its assets, such as the land and the building, may indeed have a length life longer than the life of the shareholders.

Disadvantages of the corporation are that, depending on its size and number of owners, decision-making can be a lengthy process. Dilution of control and net income can also occur if there are a great many shareholders (although this would not normally be true of the typical private company). Also, double taxation exists for shareholders of incorporated companies. The corporation pays taxes on its income at the corporate tax rate. Any after-tax income may be distributed to the individual shareholders by way of dividends. The individual is then taxed for these dividends at personal tax rates.

For more information about incorporating, see the *Incorporation and Business Guide* for your province, published by Self-Counsel Press.

4

PREPARE YOURSELF
FOR THE FRANCHISOR

In the last chapter, you tried a short questionnaire to help determine whether or not you should go into business for yourself. In this chapter, you are going to investigate yourself even further in order to know what is expected of you as a possible franchisee and whether or not you will be able to perform to the expectations of the franchisor. (In the next two chapters, we will take a look at what you should expect from a franchisor.)

Before starting out on your franchise hunt, you should be aware of your personal qualifications to be a franchisee in the type of franchise you have in mind. Are you genuinely enthusiastic? Do you have the ability, both physically and emotionally, that is required to develop a successful business? Some franchisor advertisements tend to make you believe that through part-time work, or absentee ownership, you can make a fortune in franchising. Experience shows success only happens with hard work and a full-time effort. Are you willing to accept this with a product or service, and a franchisor, that you may be locked in to for many years? If the answer to these questions is "yes," then you should proceed with the next step: finding the franchisors.

a. FINDING THE FRANCHISORS

One source of franchisor contact is newspaper advertisements, usually placed in the business section or in the business opportunities section of the classified advertisements. Business journals are also a good source of franchisor advertisements.

Sometimes, business opportunity shows, often held in hotels in larger cities, can be a source of franchisor

26

shows are franchisors and can provide literature and information about their franchise systems.

A third source is a franchise directory, which lists franchisors' names and addresses, information on the type of franchise, the costs involved, and other useful information. You can obtain a directory of Canadian franchisors from —

International Franchise Opportunities
9 Duke Street
P.O. Box 670
St. Catherines, Ontario
L2R 6W8

Franchise consultants, if there are any in your town or city (check the telephone directory Yellow Pages) can be a useful source of ideas on franchises. However, since they frequently earn their fees from franchisors, they might tend to recommend only those franchisors from whom they would receive a seller's commission.

b. THE FRANCHISOR'S QUESTIONS ABOUT YOU

You must understand that any franchisor you approach will want to find out who you are. More than likely you will have to complete a questionnaire similar to one you might complete if you were filling out a job application. However, the franchisor's questionnaire will include questions about your financial affairs (as well as, perhaps, your spouse's) and details about your personal assets and net worth.

The reason for this is that many new small businesses fail because of initial underfinancing and the inability of the owner/operator to fall back on personal assets to carry the business for the first six months or, in some cases, the first year.

A franchisor will want to know if you have previously been self-employed. If you have, this demonstrates that you have experience in small business management and have endured the feeling of surviving on your own. Despite this experience, a franchisor may still question you about your interest in receiving further training in their particular line of business. Any reluctance by you at this point may indicate an insincerity on your part about living up to the franchisor's expectations of you.

1. Past experience

In some cases, the type of experience that you have had will be important to the franchisor. For example, if you have worked in a restaurant for 10 years and have learned the ropes as an employee, your desire to invest in a restaurant franchise might be obvious.

The first types of franchise that you should investigate are those in areas in which you already have had experience or exposure (unless, of course, you didn't like what you were doing).

However, a desire to break out of previous experience into being your own boss may not appeal to a franchisor as a desirable characteristic if you stress it too strongly. Your concern for business autonomy can work against you, since in many franchises the individual operation is not a separate business but part of a larger system. To the franchisor, you must fit into that larger system. Uniformity of operation is where most of the advantages of the franchise system of operation pay off, and from that point of view you may not be your own boss.

For example, as a completely autonomous business operator starting out in business for yourself you might find that, after a few months, a product line that you are carrying is not selling well and you may decide to drop it and replace it with another one that you wish to try. In franchising, your contract with the franchisor may not permit this type of entrepreneurship, experimentation, and individuality. If a franchisor is advertising a specific product or products, then you will generally have no choice about carrying them. Even though you are the owner of the franchise, as far as the franchisor is concerned you are really only the owner/manager of that outlet.

In addition, just as you are generally viewed as the employee as far as the franchisor is concerned, you will also have employees who must conform to standards. Again, these standards may not be your own. In running your own independent business, you may be able to manage your employees in an unorthodox, but successful, way because of your personality. But a franchisor expects your employees to perform to the franchisor's standards and methods of operation, and not those that you would otherwise implement.

You will likely be asked questions about whether or not you consider the purchase of the franchise as a long-term investment to see if you are in it for a fast return on your investment. The franchisor will try to determine if you are interested in this type of business and whether or not you are really enthusiastic and determined to make it a success. Don't forget, the franchisor has an investment in you, which will not pay off if you fail. If the franchisor thinks you will fail, you won't even be given the opportunity to try to be successful.

2. Spouse's financial situation

Earlier in this chapter, it was mentioned that the franchisor would probably ask questions about your spouse's financial situation. The franchisor is interested in this for a number of reasons. In fact, you may even be asked to bring your spouse (assuming you have one) to one of the initial meetings.

The franchisor will want to make sure that both of you are prepared for the commitment of both money and hard work to produce a profitable franchise. He or she may probe your willingness to work long hours, and your family's approval of this. Do you have their moral support? Do they think you will be successful? In fact, not only should the franchisor be interested in the answers to these questions, but so should you.

You must understand that the franchisor's interest in you, your background, your family's support, your motivation, your financial resources, your previous business experience, and similar matters are primarily to protect the franchisor's and your investment. However, despite this concern on the part of the franchisor, remember that all this probing cannot guarantee success regardless of how hard you, and your family, work. Risk may be reduced through the franchising approach to business, but it is not eliminated.

3. A word of caution

Finally, a word of caution. Many unethical franchise sellers have used the "interest in the franchisee" approach for their own profitable ends. For example, franchisors have been known to expose potential franchisees to batteries of difficult tests and to question them about all kinds of personal matters such as religious beliefs, credit ratings, standing in the community, and other similar things. The only motivation for this is to convince you that the franchisor is very serious about ensuring that you would be a good franchisee. Then, when you have "passed" all tests with flying colors, you will not be able to resist signing up.

Therefore, do not be rushed into signing any contract following such "investigations," particularly if they are accompanied by offers of exclusive territory rights if you sign now before they are offered to other franchisee applicants (or other similar come ons).

Remember that, even though the franchisor is investigating you, you have a similar right to investigate the franchisor. Reputable franchisors expect you to take your time. In fact, they should welcome this since it shows you are serious about your interest in franchising and not prone to unpredictable, unconsidered decision making.

c. HOW LONG WILL IT TAKE?

After you begin your search, it can take weeks, sometimes even months, if a suitable site has to be found or a lease negotiated, to actually sign a franchise contract.

In some cases, strong and popular franchisors have waiting lists of prospective franchisees so that one or more years may pass before you can be in business with that franchisor. However, take advantage of whatever time element is involved to ensure that each move you make is the right one.

Franchising is a two-way street. It has benefits to both franchisor and franchisee. In the same way that the franchisor investigates you, you should take the same time to investigate the franchisor. In the next two chapters, we shall see some ways this can be done.

5

CHECKING OUT THE FRANCHISE

a. KNOWING THE LANGUAGE

Before you begin, you should know the language of franchising. As you know by now, the franchisor is the person granting the franchise and offering the business expertise, while the franchisee is the person acquiring the right to operate the business.

However, in some franchising relationships, the operator who buys the right to run the business is called a licensee. This implies that he or she has a licence to use the name of the product, service, or trademark involved, but is not given an established system of operating the business.

Another form of licence arrangement is a dealership. Again, there would be no set system of operation involved, and possibly not even a trademark. Generally, a dealership involves only the sale of a product or products (rather than a service, or a service and a product) such as, for example, an automobile dealership. Similarly, a distributorship is similar to a dealership, except that it is generally at the wholesale level. Some dealerships and distributorships are available on a part-time basis, but they would then probably generate only part-time earnings.

The franchise that you will probably most likely be involved in (if you want to run your own full-time franchised business) is commonly known as a business format franchise, where you agree to run the business according to a format or system established by the franchisor (right down to the uniforms of employees, or the method used to wash the floor) in order to maintain the integrity, and the profit, of the franchisor.

b. FRANCHISE PROMOTIONS

The following is an actual advertisement:

A low initial investment will give you an exclusive franchise territory with unlimited profit potential. A full time income with only part-time effort. No previous experience needed. We provide you with intensive training and supervision to guarantee immediate success.

Sounds too good to be true? It probably is, but advertisements like that have trapped many an unwary franchisee investor over the years. Such advertisements promising blatantly overoptimistic profits for little work; brochures that misrepresent the real earning power of the franchise; failure of franchisors to produce promised assistance, products or services; and the sale of virtually nonexistent franchise packages are among the deceptions that have disillusioned franchisee investors.

Dishonest promoters have also been known to use a franchise name or trademark deceptively like that of a well-known franchisor. You should be sure that you are indeed dealing with the particular franchise company that you are interested in and that the individual you are dealing with has the authority to act on its behalf.

You should be particularly wary of any franchise situation where:

(a) You are promised high profits for minimum effort.

(b) The franchisor is hesitant to give you the names of other franchisees, or similar references.

(c) Your questions are not answered directly.

(d) Specific examples of the types of training and management assistance are not given.

(e) You are discouraged from having your lawyer review the contract.

(f) You are pressured to sign the contract immediately with the threat that otherwise the opportunity will no longer be available.

(g) You have the impression the franchisor is more interested in selling you the franchise than having you run a successful business.

(h) Rapid growth rates are projected, such as from 10 franchise operations now to double that next year, and 500 in five years. This type of rapid growth (if it happens) can lead to severe management and financial problems, and the individual franchise may not be particularly successful.

Although most franchises are managed by reputable people, even among those there will still be some that are poorly managed and financially insecure.

c. INVESTIGATE THE FRANCHISOR

A good franchisor will ask a lot of questions about you, and you should be prepared for them as indicated before. But, by the same token, you should have just as many questions, if not more, to ask about the franchisor.

For example, when was the company started and how long was it in business before it started franchising? The answer to this question will tell you whether the product or the franchising came first; if the company was successful with its product before franchising, it is likely to be successful with franchising.

How many franchises does the company have and how are they spread geographically? This will show you, in conjunction with the date that the company started franchising, whether or not its franchising has grown gradually or not. A gradual pattern of growth and geographical spread indicates a more stable situation. Generally, a newer franchise will have most of its franchises clustered around its home location, whereas a franchisor in business for several years who claims to be national will have franchises spread across the country.

However, you should not make a decision about the franchisor based on size. A small but relatively unknown franchise system may be well managed. Relatively few franchisors, including some of the most successful, are really big. The fact that a franchisor has a business in only one region or market area does not mean that you should preclude signing up for it in that region or in another area. A franchisor that is successful now in that region could well become equally successful in other areas, or even nationwide, particularly if market conditions elsewhere are similar.

1. What to look for

As a wise prospective franchisee, you should be looking for a franchisor who has been carrying on a successful business for at least several years or who can demonstrate the ability to produce a successful business over the coming years. It is up to you to investigate the particular franchisor(s) that you are interested in. Even if the franchisor is a public company with a stock exchange listing, this is no guarantee. Investigation by you is still required.

You should beware of a corporation that is merely a "shell" with no significant assets and thus nothing you can sue for if you endure financial losses due to the actions or inactions of the franchisor. Similarly, be careful of purchasing a franchise from a franchisor with no assets or operating base in Canada since any legal actions then become both more expensive and more difficult.

If you can obtain financial statements showing the asset base of the franchisor, make sure they are audited ones since this is an added security concerning their authenticity. In checking the financial statements, or having your accountant check them, see if the major income of the franchisor is from initial franchise fees rather than ongoing royalties. If so, this may indicate the franchisor is in business to sell franchises rather than to develop a franchising system.

Is the franchisor a comparatively small enterprise, a national company, or a multinational company? Find out who the franchise principals are and what their track record is. Is their business history connected to the product or service they are franchising? If the answer is no, you may not be able to depend on them for expertise in running your franchise.

Find out if the franchisor is an independent company, or part of a larger company. If it is part of a larger company that can be important to you in terms of financial stability and visibility, and it helps when you go looking for financing.

2. Private or public company?

Is the company you are dealing with a proprietorship, a partnership, or an incorporated company? For many reasons an incorporated company would be preferable. In that case, determine if you are dealing with a private or a public incorporated company.

If it is private, you may have difficulty obtaining financial background information. If it is a public company registered with a stock exchange, you can easily obtain financial information about the company from any stockbroker. This information will indicate trends in sales, profits, and earnings per share and also details concerning the principals involved. If you don't have access to a broker, most libraries have reference volumes that contain information about most public companies.

Also, if the company is a public one, you should be able to obtain a copy of its prospectus, which will provide you with a lot of the answers to your questions.

If the company is a private one, ask the franchisor for bank and major supplier references whom you can contact for opinions about the franchisor's financial stability.

Other sources where you can obtain assistance in checking the franchisor are —

(a) Your local Better Business Bureau

(b) The Better Business Bureau of the franchisor's head office city

(c) Your local Chamber of Commerce

(d) A Dun and Bradstreet report on the company (You should be able to obtain this report from your banker.)

(e) The Minister of Consumer and Commercial (or Corporate) Relations in your province

(f) The Association of Canadian Franchisors
150 Eglinton Avenue E.
Toronto, Ontario
M4P 1E8

(g) Deputy Director for Franchising
Alberta Securities Commission
10th Floor — 10065 Jasper Avenue
Edmonton, Alberta
T5J 3B1

36

3. Other questions

You might also want to ask the franchisor what the expansion plans are, to see if there is a set objective and a definite plan for growth. Also, if this growth is going to be rapid, will the franchisor be able to continue to provide the same level of service, advice, training, market research, and similar backup support that each individual franchisee pays for when joining the system? There is nothing wrong with growth, since it adds to national visibility of the franchise (and this, in itself, is good advertising), but the growth should be orderly.

How many franchises have failed; and have any failed in the past couple of years? If there have been failures, but none recently, this could mean that the franchisor has solved the failure problem. Otherwise, if failures are continuing, you will want to know the cause if the franchisor is willing to tell you. If you can obtain the names and addresses or telephone numbers of franchisees who have failed it would be a good idea to talk to one or two of them to see if their explanation for failure coincides with the franchisor's reason. If there is disagreement you will have to use your own good sense to draw conclusions. Alternatively, you could contact the local Better Business Bureau in the town or city of the failed franchise to see if they have an explanation.

4. Why does the franchisor go into franchising?

One question that you might have is why the franchisor does not operate all of the franchise branches if the business is a successful one. The answer is that the franchisor/franchisee arrangement is a good way to expand the franchisor's business, rather than opening up branch operations with managers in charge. The franchisor is counting on the franchisee's investment of capital plus entrepreneurial initiative to provide more profits than would be the case with a branch operation. Individuals who have invested their own money in a business are often more willing to put in the time to make it successful for themselves than would a paid manager.

This raises another question. Why can't you buy a franchise and have a manager run it? The answer is that you can, unless the franchise agreement/contract prohibits absentee ownership. However, with many franchises you would probably find that you could not afford to take this approach since the return on your investment, after deducting the manager's salary, would not make it worthwhile. However, franchisees who start out with one franchise, and then add others (where the franchisor/franchisee contract permits this) will often find that with growth they must hire unit managers and, in some cases, area managers.

5. Franchisor owned outlets

One other question you might want to raise with the franchisor is whether or not all outlets are franchised. In other words, are some franchisor owned? In the latter case, find out if it is because they have been repurchased by the franchisor and, if so, how recently. If there is evidence of a repurchase plan, check the contract to see what repurchase price guarantees you have. If repurchases are because of marginal operations, or contract violations, these could indicate the franchisor's concern for strong, independent franchisees, and the franchisor's ability to keep on top of these situations.

Ask the franchisor about the inspection system. Is there one? How frequently are units inspected? What does the inspector look for?

Finally, ask the franchisor if there is a franchisee advisory council made up of elected franchisee representatives. If there is one, contacting a member of this committee may be of great help in advising you of the franchisor's system.

d. OTHER FRANCHISEES

Obtain from the franchisor a list of other franchisees, preferably in your local area. Be wary of a franchisor who does not willingly give you their names and addresses. Talk to these other franchisees, particularly the ones who have been in business for several years and in towns or cities whose market size (population) is similar to the market size where you might be locating. Ask for their views on the franchisor. You might want to be guided by the following questions:

(a) What was the total investment (not just the down payment) required by the franchisor, and were there any unexpected or hidden costs?

(b) Were the financial projections of revenue, expenses, and profit by the franchisor accurate?

(c) Did the franchisor live up to his or her promises in such matters as assistance in opening the business and advertising and promotional support?

(d) What was the extent and nature of training provided, and was it adequate?

(e) Is the product supplied by the franchisor of good quality and are deliveries promptly made?

(f) How long did it take for the business to reach its break-even point, and how much longer before it could support you?

(g) Have you had disagreements with the franchisor? If so, how were they settled, and were you satisfied?

(h) What periodic reports do you have to send to the franchisor, and is there useful feedback?

(i) Would you advise anyone to start a franchise with this particular franchisor?

(j) If you could change anything in the contract what would it be?

Too many franchisees start in business and wait until they are in trouble before talking to other franchisees. Don't make this mistake. However, remember that some unethical franchisors may direct you to their most successful franchisees. Try to find some who may not be as successful. However, in one case, some unhappy franchisees were told by the franchisor to speak favorably about the company so that the businesses of these unhappy franchisees could then be sold to prospective franchisees. Some franchisors use this tactic (known as "churning") to repeatedly sell the same franchise location to a succession of franchisees each of whom fails because of the basically unprofitable nature of the franchise in that particular location. Each new franchisee is not made aware of the true situation, or else is convinced that he or she could do a better job than all predecessors.

Remember that, to the franchisor, the best franchisee is the one who can understand and operate within the franchise system without trying to change it. In talking to franchisees you may come across some who want to both have and eat their cake. These are ones with no previous business experience who relied on the franchisor's expertise to start out with a successful system. As they gain experience, they then want to change the system by such things as discontinuing the franchisor's products, or adding new ones of their own. This can erode the whole franchise concept.

The franchisee who needs the franchisor when starting in business will in all likelihood continue to need the franchisor even if business is very profitable. For example, the franchisor can provide the market research that the individual franchisee cannot. When McDonald's saw that its traditional market was being eroded, it was market research that showed that going into the breakfast business could turn that situation around, and, more recently, it was market research that came up with the idea of the Egg McMuffin.

If you can, work in one of the other franchised operations to help determine if it is a good investment and to allow you a better perspective on what it takes to be successful in that franchise.

e. THE PRODUCT

Many franchises on the market are for service businesses. Others are for both services and products, while yet others are solely for a product or products. For convenience, where the word product is used from now on it also includes the word service.

Unless this is a brand new franchise company, your first requirement is to find out everything about the product you will be dealing with. For example, is the product manufactured by the franchisor or a third party? Is the product one for which there is likely to be a long-term demand, or is it just a fad item or one geared to a specific age group? What you have to watch for is a potential declining market. One that is still growing or one that is stable can still be a profitable investment. Generally, the demand for luxury items tends to be less certain than the demand for staple items, particularly in times of economic instability.

Remember that the franchisor's advertisements may be first class, but the product or service may be mediocre or not even suited to the area for which you might obtain the franchise.

Is the product price competitive and is its quality worth the price so that repeat customers will be encouraged? Would you buy the product and be satisfied with it at that price? Who establishes the product price, you or the franchisor? More than likely it will be the franchisor.

Is the product needed in your area and does it have year round appeal? Some products that sell well in one area may not be easily transplanted. Check to see if you have to carry specific products from the franchisor, and at what cost. Must you specify minimum quantities when ordering, and what happens if the franchisor cannot supply you? What payment terms are required? If it is only a seasonal product, or one that relies on, for example, tourists, can you survive the slack period?

Are there any government standards and regulations governing the product? If so does it meet those standards? Are there any restrictions on its use? Is the product safe, protected, and guaranteed? If a guarantee or warrantee is involved, obtain a copy and determine what your obligations and responsibilities as a franchisee are. If the product is one subject to possible breakdown, who pays for its repair? If the product is patented, you should ensure that the patents can be assumed by you.

Some products or services carry the name of a well known person. If so, try to determine if that person is simply a figurehead or actually has an investment in the business. Does the person also invest time and effort in promoting the product to everyone's benefit? Do not be attracted to a product or service simply on the basis of an important name or personality.

How is the product or service sold? Some franchises may require cold door-to-door selling. A bad debt collection agency may require telephone contact. An accounting or tax completion service, or a retail store franchise requires the customers to come to you.

Does the product or service require one specific sales method or a combination of methods? Depending on the method used you may have to provide your own sales leads, or they may be provided by the franchisor (for example, through national advertising for a restaurant). However, even in the latter case, it is important to remember that satisfied customers are your best sales lead since they provide repeat business and good word of mouth advertising.

What products or services does the franchisor plan to add in the next year or two? Future growth of the chain, and of individual franchisees, is important, as is the need to change products or services as the market demand changes (remember McMuffin). In some cases the franchisor may not provide you with this information since it may be confidential and if commonly known give the competition an edge. In that case, can you determine from your own observations of the franchisor's history that efforts have been made to keep in tune with change?

Will you have to sell any new products or services that may be introduced into the market by the franchisor in the future? Alternatively, will you be allowed to sell products or services other than from the franchisor if you wish to do so at some time in the future?

f. SUMMARY

In this chapter, you had a fairly in-depth look at some of the franchisor, franchisee, and product situations that you should explore for any franchises you may be interested in. In the next chapter, we will continue this exploration with a number of other matters you should find out about.

6

MORE CHECKING

In the preceding chapter, you saw the importance of checking out the franchisor, other franchisees in the system, and the basic product(s) involved. In this chapter we will continue this investigation with other items that you need to check out.

a. FEES, ROYALTIES, AND OTHER COSTS

Determine what the total initial franchise fee is and what you receive for it. Does the price cover just the right to use a name or trademark, or are you also buying start up inventory, equipment, and fixtures? What does any down payment fee cover? Who pays any costs resulting from delays in getting started? Whose responsibility is it to pay for legal fees and other costs, such as for permits, licences, and insurance? Does the initial fee include a deposit on the land and/or building construction? If the premises are on a leased basis from the franchisor, are there any advance payments or a damage deposit included in the fee? When are fee payments to be made?

Is any of the initial fee refundable? Some franchisors make it feasible for you to recover part or all of the initial fee if the franchise becomes successful and maintains a predetermined sales level. This is offered as an incentive to franchisees. Perhaps you can even negotiate this and have it written into the contract.

What ongoing advertising service charges and/or royalties are there? On what are they based? Generally they are a percentage of sales revenue. Find out if these continuing charges or royalties are reasonable and what the franchisor is offering in return by way of services (for example, accounting, and updated merchandising). When are payments to be made?

43

Are the franchisor's initial fee and royalty charges reasonable? Since the franchisor operates, as you will do, on establishing a price based on supply and demand for the product, the answer (in the case of a well established franchisor) is probably yes. The real question is whether or not the franchisor's asking price is worth it to you to become an operator in your own right. That question (particularly in the case of a new franchise system) may only be answerable after you are in business.

Be very careful when discussing initial fees with the franchisor. Different words or terms mean different things to different franchisors. For example, initial fee, initial cost, and total cost may mean different things. Similarly, cash required, initial cash required, down payment, investment, and equity investment can all mean the same — or all mean something different depending on the franchisor.

In trying to determine the total costs that will be required (apart from initial fees and the cost of finding, buying or leasing the land and/or building and obtaining all necessary licences and/or permits), do not overlook the cash you will need for initial working capital (money needed to pay the bills for such items as payroll, insurance, and your own salary until cash starts coming in).

b. FRANCHISOR'S ADVERTISING

Discuss the franchisor's local, regional, or national advertising program. Remember, the ongoing royalty fee you pay is supposed to be used in part for advertising. You therefore need reassurance from the franchisor of what advertising takes place in newspapers, magazines, or on radio and television. Proper and effective promotion may be critical to your success in the business. Ask where advertisements are running and check them out to verify their effectiveness from your own point of view.

Note that any local advertising that you may be allowed to do (such as direct mail) will generally be at your own cost. Any local advertising should support the franchisor's advertising, and for this reason the franchisor may supply packaged programs for your use, such as radio scripts, television commercials, and sample publicity releases. In particular find out what, if any, opening day advertising and publicity costs the franchisor will pay for.

c. LOCATION, LAYOUT, AND EQUIPMENT

Who decides the location of the franchise — you or the franchisor? What site location help will the franchisor offer (the next chapter will cover site location)? If the franchisor finds the site, make sure you are still satisfied with it.

Do your premises have to meet certain franchisor standards such as street frontage or minimum square metre area in size? Are you allowed to adapt an existing building or must you operate in newly constructed premises? If you can operate in adapted premises, and the building appearance must be changed to a standard appearance to conform to the franchise image, find out who pays for this conversion. What layout design restrictions are there? Must you conform to a detailed franchisor plan, or is there some flexibility in adapting to local conditions?

If a new building must be built, do you build and pay for it (to the franchisor's specifications), or does the franchisor build it and simply lease it to you? In a lease situation, can you move your franchise to another location if a more suitable site in the area arises?

Are specific equipment, furniture, and fixtures to be used? If the franchise system requires a standardized appearance, this may well be the case. In that case, must you buy these items from the franchisor, or can you shop around for a local supplier who may offer more competitive prices? Some franchisors make a great deal of money from selling equipment, furniture, and fixtures to franchisees. In some cases, it may be their motivation for being in business so watch this situation carefully. If you buy or, alternatively, lease the equipment and similar items from the franchisor, what is the equipment repair situation? In other words, who pays for maintenance and repair?

Most franchise agreements require you to keep the building, equipment, and furnishings in a good state of repair. The agreement also normally requires you to replace worn out or obsolete equipment with franchisor specified replacement items when necessary. The franchisor normally also specifies how, and how frequently, the building interior and exterior are to be maintained. However, you should make sure that there is some upper limit on how much must be spent on such replacement equipment and building maintenance, otherwise you could be spending unreasonably high amounts to please the franchisor without any direct return to you. The upper limit could be either a dollar amount per year or an annual percentage of revenue.

d. TRAINING

Ask what training is offered. Is it a once only arrangement for you as the franchisee, or does it include ongoing training for employees? If so, who pays this ongoing cost? Find out whether or not training will be provided to cover routine supervisory employee turnovers, as well as other employee turnovers. What is its cost, if any, to you or is it included in the initial and ongoing fees? How will you and your supervisory employees be kept up to date on new products and/or service methods? Who pays this cost?

For the ethical franchisor, training has important implications for both of you, since proper training can improve your motivation and thus increase the return to the franchisor. The actual training provided, if any, will depend on the type of franchise system and the skill level required of employees. For example, the training period required for a franchise in home improvement may require only a few days, or at the most a week or so, whereas the training required for a complex restaurant franchise could be in weeks.

In some cases, the promised training provided is inadequate and does not overcome the inexperience of the franchisee. The type of training you receive should include some or all of the following:

(a) Operating system and methods

(b) Methods of advertising and promotion

(c) Personnel management, including how to recruit and train your own employees

(d) Building and equipment maintenance

(e) Financial control procedures

e. FRANCHISOR CONTROLS

You will want to find out what controls the franchisor plans to exercise. Controls, or standardization, are the glue that bonds many franchise systems together. Most franchisors exercise this control in order to influence their own eventual profits. As the franchisee, you may perceive yourself as an independent businessperson. However, the franchisor's success is dependent on the image of the franchise system as perceived by the franchise customers. If the system does not have a product that is consistent in appearance, quality, service, or price, many of the franchise system's advantages are lost. In other words, the market image is an essential ingredient of the franchise concept.

The controls that a franchisor may use could include any or all of the following:

(a) Architectural design and layout of the franchise outlet

(b) Insurance requirements

(c) The source of equipment and furnishings required

(d) Where you may buy the product or the ingredients in the product

(e) The product quality and/or service

(f) The retail price of the product

(g) Hours of operation

(h) Parking space requirements

(i) Advertising and promotion delivery methods for the product or service

(j) Training requirements for each new employee

(k) Accounting procedures and required reports (and possibly even franchisor access to your accounting and banking records)

(l) The right of the franchisor to have the last word in any disagreements between the two of you

Generally, controls are implemented for the good of all franchisees (and, obviously, for the good of the franchisor). Sometimes, unfortunately, controls are imposed for the sole benefit of the franchisor. For example, there have been cases of franchisees following controls to the letter, building up the business, and then finding that the franchisor could terminate the agreement and continue to reap the profits.

In a similar vein, franchisees have found that their "exclusive" territorial rights are not sufficiently protected in the contract to ensure that the franchisor does not open up a competitive operation on the other side of the street (the question of territory will be discussed in a later chapter on the contract).

f. CONTINUED MANAGEMENT ASSISTANCE

You will probably be better off with a franchisor who can show evidence of continued management assistance after opening. This may include ongoing management or employee training, new merchandising ideas, and new products. Management assistance should also include visits by the franchisor or a representative to your premises. Find out the frequency of these visits.

Also, is there any assurance that head office personnel will be available for consultation when unusual problems arise? This should be provided since you should be able to look to the head office in the same way as a branch manager of a company would look to the head office.

What kind of backup management help does the franchisor have in the head office? Are there specialists who have worked in the field themselves? Are there accounting and finance experts, as well as specialists in areas such as site selection, construction supervision, marketing, advertising and promotion, personnel and training, operations, real estate, and research and development? Only a larger franchisor will be able to afford specialists in each of these areas.

If you were going with a smaller, newer franchise, you might still want to ensure there was some general experience with the concept. For example, if it were a new motel franchise, at least one of the principals involved should have had experience in operating motels.

g. FRANCHISOR UNIQUENESS

Ask if there are any unique aspects to the franchisor's system and if there is a cost to you for them. Also, what employee benefit plans does the franchisor offer (if any), such as life insurance, medical insurance, and retirement plans?

h. BEWARE OF PYRAMIDING

Be particularly alert to the pyramiding form of franchising. Initially, pyramiding may seem like another form of franchise distribution, but it is, in fact, in conflict with both legitimate franchising and, in most cases, the law.

Pyramid franchisors, or operators, are basically take-your-money-and-run operators who disappear quickly when the pyramid is close to collapsing. The pyramid approach uses high pressure salespersons who emphasize the benefits that can accrue from recruiting others to distribute a product. The franchisee buys a right to distribute the product, but it is made clear to you that you can also make money (in many cases, more money) by recruiting new distributors. For each new distributor that you, as a franchisee, find, you may be promised half of the new recruit's investment money, which encourages you to forget the product that is supposed to be the basis of the franchise system.

For this reason it is easy to smell out pyramid schemes; when the emphasis is on recruiting new members, rather than selling the product, you are into a pyramid scam, and the sooner you get out the better.

In particular, watch for franchise sellers who have rented fancy offices for short periods, or suites in luxury hotels, and who run expensive, glowing newspaper or other advertisements to pull in prospective franchisees. In many cases, these pyramid promoters promise more than they can produce, but by the time you find out the real situation their promises are worthless since they have, so to speak, flown the coop.

i. FINANCIAL FORECASTS

One of the key elements indicating the success of a new franchise operation, particularly if it is part of a new franchise system, is the forecasting accuracy of the financial data.

In many businesses, there is a two-year rule of thumb. This rule of thumb says that it normally takes two years for the business to break even, or achieve that point where revenue covers all costs but provides no profit. A franchise should, however, break even much sooner than two years since you are paying for proven products, systems, and procedures.

Unfortunately, misleading profit claims are one of the most prevalent deceptive ploys of dishonest franchisors. A great many franchisees who failed have failed because their net income figures were not only below the maximum income projections of the franchisor, but also below average figures provided, and some even below minimum figures.

Therefore, even if you obtain projected sales revenue and expense forecasts from the franchisor (and you should), take them with a grain of salt until you have had a chance, with your accountant, to make whatever verifications of them are possible.

Your accountant, just like your lawyer, should be one who is both well versed in small business operations and also one who is familiar with franchised businesses. If possible, obtain an accountant who is familiar with the business that you have a particular interest in (for example, a service company, a retail store, a restaurant).

In particular, you should try to verify the figures you receive with other franchisees in the same system whose business volume should be approximately the same as yours. However, remember that sales and expense figures can seldom be duplicated from one location to another since conditions do vary.

1. Some financial questions

For any income and expense statement provided by the franchisor, find out if the statement is an actual or an estimated one. Preferably, statements should be actual. If they are, ask if they are based on a franchisee operated business or one operated by the franchisor personally. It can make a difference since, in a franchisor operated business, the franchisor may not show an expense for royalties for advertising.

If the figures are from a franchisee operation, try to determine which one and visit it to talk to the franchisee. How does that operation compare with your own planned one as far as size of premises, market size served, and similar factors?

Are the sales figures projected attainable in your particular location? Ask an established franchisee if the figures seem realistic from his or her point of view in your location. What are some unique features of your operation that may impact sales? For example, hours of operation that differ from other franchisees?

Are operating expenses realistic? What expenses might change for your particular area or location? For example, if this were a restaurant operation, are food purchase costs to you higher or lower than in other parts of the country? Similarly, if the business requires one or several employees apart from yourself, how do different wage rates, such as the provincial minimum, affect your business compared to the figures in the statement provided by the franchisor? Does the competitive labor situation, or a union, require you to pay higher than average wage rates?

Are some expenses omitted from the franchisor statements that you would have to include on your statements? For example, would you have depreciation on your owned building whereas the statements presented to you show only a rent expense from a leased premise? Alternatively, are there some expenses you would not have that do show on the franchisor's statement?

Do the statements presented show a salary for you as a manager? If so, how much is it? Is that reasonable for the hours of work you may have to put in? Divide the salary by hours of work and calculate what your hourly wage rate is. How does that compare with the hourly rate paid to any of your employees?

What will be the return on your investment? How does that compare to investing your money in some other way? For example, what could you receive in the way of an interest rate (return on investment) by leaving your money in the bank?

Will the cash flow from the business be sufficient to cover your cash requirements until the business is well established? Will you be able to pay off long-term debts (such as a mortgage on the building) without additional financing?

2. In summary

Since the variety and type of franchised operations is so broad, it is impossible to provide you with every possible question that could be asked concerning the financial statements. Each type of franchise requires a different set of questions, but it is hoped that those posed above will set you on the right track and provide you with a basic reference point. No doubt, in your particular case you, or your accountant, should be able to pose questions that are appropriate in the circumstances.

7

SITE SELECTION

Although site selection may not seem very important to a franchised business, particularly one that caters primarily to pedestrian traffic, location can make or break any franchised operation. In fact, location is probably the most important factor for success unless you are operating some sort of dealership or distributorship that allows you to do business from your home. In that case, you might choose to skip this chapter.

Statements made about suitable locations are frequently accompanied by rules of thumb. Beware of rules of thumb. For example, one rule of thumb in a motel location situation is that it should be on the right-hand side of the road. This is fine if the motel is to attract potential customers as they approach a community that they are planning to stay in overnight. But many travellers prefer to drive through a community and stay on its far side overnight so that they can be on the highway early to continue their travels the next day. To such customers a convenient motel on the right (as they exit the centre of the community) is on the left for those approaching from the other direction.

Other rules of thumb, such as buying where land is cheap or where traffic noise and commotion are minimized, should be treated with similar caution since it has been proved many, many times that a business built in a supposedly poor location according to a rule of thumb can become a highly-successful enterprise.

a. SELECTING LOCATION

Perhaps a more practical general rule of thumb is to select a location that suits the needs of the customers who are, or are expected to be, the market for your business. You should become familiar with the specifics of the franchise you are interested in to understand its particular site and market requirements.

In some cases, the franchisor will provide these services, since the franchisor is as interested in you having a good location as you are. But an independent survey of the site might be worth the cost. Although the franchisor is supposed to be capable of selecting locations, the opinion of a location consultant (and most large accounting firms have specialists in this area) does not hurt as a double check.

If the franchisor does not provide this service, you are on your own and will have to approach a site location specialist. The services of site selection companies include analysis of population density, customer profiles, access and traffic flows, the drawing power of other businesses in the area, visibility of business and signs, the average sale you should be able to do per square metre, and what effect any nearby competitors will have. Note, though, that assessing a commercial location is both complex and tricky. It is more art than science, and even the specialists can be wrong. It has been estimated that about 20% of locations do not perform as expected.

Even though you may rely on the franchisor or a site location specialist to help with site selection there are some obvious things that you should be aware of. For example, you would not want to locate in an area populated or frequented by people of a different socio-economic base than you must sell your product or service to.

Similarly, you would not want to locate a particular type of restaurant in an area that is populated with people whose ethnic background is not oriented to the type of food you will be selling; nor would you want to locate a business geared to selling to the younger generation in an area inhabited by older married couples.

A good location is frequently one near another store that is successfully attracting the kind of people you need as a market base. Sometimes a difference of 15 or 20 metres in location can have a drastic impact, one way or another, on sales. This is particularly true of shopping centre or shopping mall locations. For example, if you are selling impulse items in a shopping mall, a location close to the main traffic flow at the entrance to a major department store or by an escalator, would be better than at the end of a corridor that, comparatively, is never busy.

b. VISIBILITY, ACCESSIBILITY, AND SUITABILITY

Three extremely important aspects of site location are visibility, accessibility, and suitability. Each of these will be discussed briefly.

1. Visibility

Visibility of the business may be more important to the customer who arrives at your front door by automobile than it is for the pedestrian, but even for the pedestrian visibility is still important.

Poor visibility of a business outlet can be improved by appropriate outdoor advertising signs that can both attract attention and give directions. This is especially true in a location where the business might be surrounded by larger and taller buildings and where such problems as one-way streets and other complications can confuse the customer travelling by car.

2. Accessibility

A second factor in site location is accessibility, again particularly for those arriving by automobile. An ideal situation is where traffic flow in and around the site minimizes the effects of such things as left turn restrictions that prevent the motorist from easily approaching the business.

Equally important is a knowledge about future street and/or highway changes that could change a desirable access situation into an undesirable one.

If a routing from the main travel stream is difficult, and sign ordinances prohibit providing the motorist with information such as where to turn to reach the business, then an infinitely large number of potential customers may be lost.

3. Suitability

Even for a site with good visibility and easy access, a critical factor is the suitability of the site. For many businesses, such as a restaurant, a motel, or a building supply outlet, **the greatest site limitation is space for parking.** The space required for parking is usually greater than that required for the building.

Other questions are: Is the site reasonably flat and free of rock outcroppings that might be expensive to remove or build around? Is road frontage adequate? Is there sufficient soil depth for the building so that large quantities of fill are not required? These are typical of the questions that need to be asked about the site and its suitability.

c. BYLAWS AND SIMILAR PROBLEMS

Before going too far with planning a business on what seems a desirable site, it is best to make sure that all the local bylaws, such as zoning restrictions, building codes, fire regulations, and similar laws, will allow you to build the type of building you have in mind or that the franchisor requires you to have. For example, if zoning does not allow the construction of a restaurant on the site, or if there are height restrictions, can you get a change in zoning (a variance) from the local government?

Sign ordinances should also be checked to determine if there are any restrictions on type, placement, number, and size of signs. Make sure that the information obtained concerning bylaws and ordinances is up to date since changes do occur in these regulations from time to time.

A check with the local engineering or public works department will provide information about the present suitability of sewers, water mains, and electrical power supplies. If these are not adequate for the size of building planned, the cost to upgrade them could be prohibitive.

The proximity of connection points for utility services is also important since the cost to hook up to one or more of these services that might be several hundred metres away could be exorbitant.

The highways department should be approached to provide information concerning their future plans for new highways and/or by-pass routes that could severely affect the visibility and accessibility factors of the business. For example, if the business is on a two-lane highway that is slated for widening to four lanes, is a divider planned for separating the two halves of the highway? If this is the case, it may make it difficult, if not impossible, for arriving or departing motorists to drive directly into or out of the property.

The land deed should be checked to see what easements or other restrictions there are. Are there any buildings on the land that will first have to be demolished? If so, this cost of demolition must be added to the asking price for the land.

d. EXPANSION

Expansion potential is a necessary part of site selection. Even though present plans are for a specific size of building to meet current or immediately anticipated needs, you should think about growth in demand in the future.

Even if investment cash does not currently allow buying more land than is immediately needed, it might be a good idea to select a site with adjacent land that could, in the future, be available for purchase.

e. PROPERTY APPRAISAL

Before making the final commitment to purchase land for a building, an appraisal is recommended. This appraisal will allow comparison of the site selected with information about similar properties in the area. If necessary, obtain a second appraisal for purposes of confirmation.

The money invested in this will ensure that the business is not located on an overpriced, unsuitable site.

f. SUMMARY

In summary, selecting the right site involves skill, common sense, knowledge, good judgment, and an awareness of the requirements of a successful business, such as traffic patterns and circulation, business generators, building planning, real estate, and — probably as important as any — luck in location selection.

8

LONG-TERM FINANCING

The major requirement in financing a new business operation is for long-term funds for assets such as land and building, and, to a lesser degree, long-life fixtures and equipment. This chapter discusses such long-term financing. However, it should be noted that if you are leasing a building, or land and building, the requirement for long-term financing is considerably reduced. Also, if the type of franchise you are contemplating investing in does not require major long-term financing, you may wish to skim over some of the sections in this chapter.

Although, over time, a variety of different methods of raising long-term capital have been used by businesses, mortgage debt and owner equity have been the two most popular methods.

a. MORTGAGE FINANCING

1. Construction and development loan

In many cases, before long-term mortgage money can be obtained, the developer of a new business requires a construction and development loan.

Construction and development loans are short-term loans (up to three years) that carry a relatively high interest rate because of their risk to the lender. Such loans are used to pay the contractors for construction of the building. Loans are usually made for up to 75% of the appraised value of land and improvements in place (less the amount of any mortgage on the property).

As construction proceeds, the lender makes advances from time to time. Only the interest is paid on such loans during this period. The loan principal is repaid when the property is in operation and ready for business out of long-term permanent mortgage funds that are advanced to the developer (usually from a different lender) at that time. The long-term mortgage may or may not be arranged at the time construction begins.

In addition, the long-term mortgage lender often requires the business to be in full operation before funds are advanced. Prior to opening, there may be additional carrying costs required by you for furniture, fixtures, equipment, inventories, and a host of other pre-opening expenses, such as advertising and staff training.

The risks are obvious, and for this reason the interest rates charged to new business operators on construction and development loans are generally one or two interest percentage points more than those that would be charged by lenders to their established commercial customers.

2. Long-term first mortgage

A mortgage is a grant, by the borrower to a creditor or lender, of preference or priority in a particular asset. If the borrower is in default (for example, for nonpayment of interest and/or principal owing), the creditor holding the mortgage is entitled to force the sale of the specific asset or assets pledged as security. Proceeds of the sale would go to the holder of the first mortgage before any other creditors would receive anything. If another creditor had a mortgage on the same asset or assets, he or she would be classified as a second mortgage holder and would rank below the first mortgage holder but above a third mortgage holder (if one existed) or other creditors of the borrower in default. The legal procedure by which the first mortgage holder can force the sale is called foreclosure.

In the business world, first mortgage lenders are generally organizations that have collected savings from many individual investors or lenders. The organization, acting as an intermediary, centralizes these savings and lends them in lump sums. Such organizations are insurance companies, pension companies, real estate investment trusts, commercial and mortgage bankers, and, in some cases, the franchisor with shareholder funds.

3. Feasibility studies and other requirements

Before lending money, these organizations would consider factors like the borrower's track record. A business operator with a proven record of five years or more of successful experience in business would be more likely to obtain funds at a reasonable rate than would a novice. However, the franchisor's track record can be important in obtaining a reduced interest rate on a mortgage.

Lenders also usually like to have feasibility studies professionally prepared and presented by an impartial third party with no vested interest in the development. The franchisor might indeed do this for you (if that is acceptable to the lender). In fact, if the franchisor is not willing to do this at his or her cost if requested to do so, you might interpret this to mean that the franchisor did not have much faith in a franchise at that location.

Also, ensure that any money that you deposit with the franchisor on the basis of having a feasibility study done is returned to you if the feasibility study is negative, i.e., shows that the franchise would likely not be successful.

Lenders are also concerned about the amount of equity invested by the owner. This equity usually takes the form of land ownership or direct cash investment in shares if the company is incorporated. Without such equity investment, the mortgage lender is taking a very high risk. Generally, such equity needs to be a minimum of 25 to 30% of total financing.

A prospective lender will also want assurance that proper accounting procedures, particularly for cost control, will be instituted. Lenders frequently require audited financial statements, sometimes as frequently as monthly. This allows them to read possible danger signs before it is too late.

Some lenders carry out on-site inspections of properties in which they have investments to ensure that the property is not being run down and that it is being maintained adequately. This ensures that their investment is better protected. In some cases, the mortgage investor may stipulate a percentage of annual revenue that must be spent on property maintenance.

The location of a new business can also be a critical consideration since so much of the revenue may be contingent on vehicle or pedestrian traffic flows, and a site study (which is often part of a feasibility study) may be required.

4. Loan terms

Generally, first mortgages can be obtained for up to 70 or 75% of the appraised value of the land and building offered as security for the loan. If the land is leased, then the mortgage would usually be obtainable only on the appraised value of the building. Loan terms usually run for a maximum of 20 to 25 years. However, the term could be as short as 10 years, particularly if the franchise contract is only that long.

Repayment of loans is generally made in equal monthly **payments of principal and interest. These payments are** calculated so that, at the stated interest rate, the regular payments will completely amortize (pay off) the mortgage by the end of its life. Sometimes the payments are calculated so that, during the early years, interest only is paid (with no reduction in principal).

5. Early prepayment

Most first mortgage loans do not permit any early prepayment for at least the first several years. Thus you are locked in for that period and cannot benefit if interest rates decline.

Where prepayment is permitted, the mortgagor may impose a penalty. The penalty is usually a percentage of the balance still owing, and the percentage may decline as time goes by. You might be prepared to pay such a penalty. For example, if the initial mortgage carried a 16% interest rate, **and current rates had declined to 14%, you might be able to** negotiate a new loan with a new lender and use part of the proceeds to pay off the remaining balance of the initial mortgage plus penalty. The penalty imposition may be more than offset by the interest reduction over the term of the new mortgage. Since circumstances in each case will differ, each decision about long-term mortgage refinancing must be made on its own merits.

6. Call provision

Just as you may be permitted such repayment opportunities to benefit from changed general market interest rates, so too is the lender usually protected. Most mortgage agreements have a call provision in them. This call provision allows the lender, after a stated number of years, to ask for complete repayment of the mortgage. The lender and borrower then renegotiate a new mortgage at a new interest rate for a further stipulated period of time. A lender would probably call a loan if interest rates had increased since the original mortgage agreement was signed.

7. Other compensation

Some lenders also require additional compensation, such as a fee, discount, or bonus. For example, a $10 000 bonus on a $250 000 mortgage would mean you receive only $240 000 but must pay back principal and interest on the $250 000. Such front-end "loads" obviously raise the effective interest rate.

Other lenders may ask for an equity participation. Such equity participation increases the lender's return on the investment and, at the same time, dilutes your return on investment. Equity might take the form of a percentage of annual revenue, or an investment in common shares.

In some cases, the lender might enter into a joint venture agreement with you. Such an agreement might provide you with some equity funds (while giving up part of equity control) as well as mortgage funds.

In other cases, the mortgage investor might supply 100% of the total project cost in exchange for a substantial equity position. This might significantly reduce your capital outlay and at the same time reduce your risk, control, and potential future income.

8. Equipment and fixtures

Most long-term mortgage lenders will not normally finance any portion of the equipment and fixtures. The prime reason is that mortgage lenders are in the long-term loan business, and furniture and equipment has a relatively short-term life. However, despite this, they will sometimes attempt to obtain a first mortgage on these chattels (in addition to the long-term mortgage on the assets that they have financed). If this does occur, the lender that has financed the furniture and equipment takes a subordinated position. In this way, a first mortgage lender who has to foreclose is sure that the furniture and equipment will not be repossessed and that the business can continue to operate.

For the same reason, mortgage lenders may prohibit the leasing of furniture and equipment (including subsequent replacements) even though this may be difficult to police.

9. Second mortgages

Second mortgages are also used for financing land and building. A second mortgage lender would take a second lien on the property mortgaged. The loan amount is generally limited to 5 to 15% of the appraised value of the property, and loan terms usually range from 5 to 15 years.

Second mortgage interest rates are generally three to four points above first mortgage rates because of the additional risk involved. Repayments are made by you over the life of the loan in equal monthly installments of principal and interest.

Excessive second mortgages can be risky to both you and the lender because of potential cash flow problems if the business is not immediately successful.

10. Personal guarantees

Finally, even if your business is incorporated, the mortgage lender(s) may require your personal guarantee of the loan in case your company does not meet its debt obligations.

b. EQUITY FINANCING

The kind of long-term financing that has been discussed so far is commonly referred to as debt financing. Debt financing is money borrowed from organizations such as banks and investment companies which do not normally have an active say in the day-to-day operation of the business. The people who do have an active say are the equity investor(s) — or the owner(s) of the company.

In order to borrow from long-term debt investors, it is normally necessary for the equity investor(s) to have a direct financial interest or investment in the business. This equity investment could range from 25 to 50% of the total investment. In fact, many franchisors stipulate a minimum 20 to 25% investment by the franchisee to cover payment for the site selection and related work done by the franchisor, the franchise fee, and start up and opening promotion costs.

This equity could come from your own savings, friends willing to invest, or even from relatives (love money).

The equity investment could be in the form of shareholder loans, or common stock or shares in the company, or a combination of loans and shares. How the owners' or equity investors' investment in the company is structured will vary in each different situation.

In particular the advice of tax accountants is suggested since your personal tax situation, and that of any other owners, and the degree of financial success of the business, can have a bearing on whether the shareholders' investment should be in the form of loans or purchase of shares.

The long-term debt investors may also place restrictions or conditions on when and how the incorporated company can pay off shareholder loans, redeem shares, or possibly even pay dividends on shares. These restrictions or conditions are imposed to protect the long-term debt investors.

9

SHORT- AND INTERMEDIATE-TERM FINANCING

In the preceding chapter, the subject of long-term financing was covered. That type of financing is primarily used for purchasing long-term assets, such as land and building, with the asset becoming the security or collateral for the debt.

In this chapter, we cover short- and intermediate-term financing. This type of financing is necessary to cover the purchases of assets having a much shorter life (such as equipment, fixtures, and furniture) and even to help pay for some other assets such as inventory.

a. SHORT-TERM FINANCING

Some of the various methods of short-term financing are discussed in the following sections.

1. Trade credit

Surprisingly, the most common means of short-term financing is trade credit. The reason for this is that most suppliers do not demand cash on delivery other than in those cases where a business has a reputation for delinquency in payment of accounts. Usually a bill or invoice for purchases is sent at the month-end. In the case of, let us say, a 30-day payment period, this would mean that you use the service or supplies received without cost for anywhere up to 60 days.

To a business, this type of trade credit is an important source of cash. Even if you have the cash to pay the bill at the time it is received, it may not be wise to do so. As long as there is no penalty imposed, you are free to let your cash sit in the bank and collect interest until the invoice has to be paid. To you this is another source of profit. This type of trade credit is sometimes called "open credit" since it is generally arranged on an understanding between buyer and seller without any formal agreement documented in writing.

There are three typical methods of arranging payment with a supplier: cash on delivery (COD), no cash discount, and cash discount.

The first, COD, in effect means that the purchaser does not receive any trade credit. Cash must be paid at the time of delivery.

The second, more common, type of arrangement is for the supplier to extend credit for a specific number of days after delivery of the goods, or after the month-end following delivery of the goods, with no cash discount permitted. In other words, the full amount of the invoice or invoices must be paid.

The third arrangement is for the supplier to offer both a credit period and a cash discount. One such common type is referred to as 2/10, net 30. This means that you are offered a 2% discount off the invoice price if the bill is paid within 10 days. If the bill is not paid within the 10-day period, it must be paid within a further 20 days but without discount. This type of arrangement is made to encourage you to pay bills promptly.

With a 2/10, net 30 arrangement, you must seriously consider the cost of not taking the discount. For example, if you make a $1000 purchase and pay within 10 days, the amount to be paid is $980. If the discount is not taken, you, in effect, have the use of this $980 for a further 20 days. However, the cost of this would be:

$$\frac{\$20}{\$980} \times \frac{365}{20} = 37.2\%$$

This is a very expensive form of financing. Even if you are short of cash, it might be wise to borrow $980 from the bank to pay within the discount period, since the bank interest expense would probably be considerably less than 37%.

2. Stretching payables

In the discussion so far, it has been assumed that you pay bills before the end of the supplier's payment period. If you delay paying beyond that date, you are using this "free" money at a further cost to the supplier. For this reason, suppliers do not encourage the practice.

Banks and other lending institutions also look unfavorably on businesses that make a habit of not paying bills promptly. If you have this reputation, you might well find that suppliers will deliver only on a COD basis. You might also find it difficult to borrow funds when needed for short-term purposes.

However, if the nature of your franchise is seasonal, you might find it difficult to pay all bills in the off season when they are due. In such cases, it might be wise to arrange for a longer payment period with suppliers whose financial resources allow them to extend longer credit. Alternatively, arrangements could be made with a lending institution to borrow funds for the interim period so that bills can be paid within the normal payment period.

You should also recognize that trade credit is not absolutely "free." The supplier who extends credit has financing costs, which must be paid out of revenue from the products sold. In other words, the cost is included in the selling price. Where competition exists among suppliers, however, this hidden cost should be minimal.

3. Short-term or operating loans

Short-term or operating loans are for financing inventory during peak periods, accounts receivable, special purchases, promotions, and other items of working capital. Normally up to 10% of annual sales can be borrowed against to finance such requirements.

The main sources of short-term loans are commercial banks or similar financial institutions. This type of loan could be secured or unsecured. The security might be any or all of the following:

(a) A fixed or floating charge debenture on inventory, equipment, or fixtures

(b) A general assignment of debts, where applicable, to finance accounts receivable

(c) An assignment of fire insurance and, in some cases, key employee life insurance

(d) A personal guarantee of you and/or your spouse when assets are registered in the spouse's name

(e) A guarantee from the franchisor

Short-term loans are usually negotiated for specific periods of time (for example 30, 60, or 90 days, and less frequently for periods up to a year or more). They may be repayable in a lump sum at the end of the period or in periodic installments, such as monthly. Each separate borrowing is usually covered by a promissory note (a form of contract spelling out the terms of the loan), and the interest rate is frequently subject to change, particularly in erratic money markets.

The interest rate is usually a stated annual interest rate. The stated rate may differ from the effective (or true) rate if the loan is discounted. Discounting means that the interest on the loan is deducted in advance. If a $1 000 bank loan is taken out at the beginning of the year, to be repaid at the end of the year at a discount (interest) rate of 15%, you would receive $850 ($1 000, less 15% of $1 000, or $150). You would repay $1 000 at the end of the year. Since you have only $850, the effective interest rate is:

$$\frac{\$150}{\$850} \times 100 = 17.6\%$$

The effective interest rate also differs from the stated rate if a loan is repayable in equal installments over the term of the loan, rather than in a lump sum at the end of the loan period as was the case above. Consider a $1 200 loan at a 12% rate, repayable in equal monthly installments of principal over a year ($100 per month) plus interest. If the interest is calculated on the initial loan, it will be 12% of $1 200, or $144 ($12 per month). The effective rate of interest will be higher than the stated 12%, however, since you do not have the use of the full $1 200 for the year.

Tables are available from which an exact rate of interest can be determined under various circumstances, but an approximate effective rate of interest can be quickly calculated. With equal monthly repayments, on average the borrower has only half the $1 200 to use over the year, or $600 ($1 200 divided by 2). The effective interest rate is then:

$$\frac{\$144}{\$600} \times 100 = 24\%$$

This is double the stated rate. In all cases where money is being borrowed, and particularly where you are shopping around for the best rate, it is important to know what the *effective* interest rate is.

4. Line of credit

A line of credit is an agreement between you and a bank specifying the maximum amount of credit (overdraft) the bank will allow you at any one time. Credit lines are usually established for one-year periods, subject to annual renegotiation and renewal.

The amount of credit is based on the bank's assessment of the creditworthiness of the company and its credit requirements.

5. Interest rates

Banks and other financial institutions vary interest rates according to money market conditions. The rates can change frequently. They also vary depending on the customer. The prime rate is generally the lowest rate available. Rates increase above that depending on the specific business, its credit rating, its size, and other factors.

It would probably not be unreasonable to suggest that most small businesses in need of bank credit would probably pay rates that tended to be among the highest. However, franchise chain operations, because of their total size and bargaining power, might be able to negotiate lower rates for their individual members, but you would probably still pay more than the prime rate.

b. INTERMEDIATE-TERM FINANCING

Somewhere between short- and long-term financing is a need at times for intermediate-term financing. A common way to obtain this financing is through term loans or through installment financing.

1. Term loans

Term loans are usually also obtained from banks or similar financial institutions, but, unlike short-term loans, are usually arranged to cover the purchase of basic inventory, leasehold improvements, and long life assets such as furniture, fixtures, and equipment. Generally 60 to 75 % of the cost of these items can be obtained through term loans. In some cases, only the interest portion of such loans is payable in the first year or two.

Term loans are usually repaid in regular installments of principal and interest over the life of the loan, which is usually less than the life of the assets for which financing is required. Term loans could vary in length from one to five years. The interest rate on term loans is usually a percentage point or more higher than that for a short-term loan made to the same borrower.

The periodic payments on term loans can be geared to the business's cash flow ability to repay. Payments could be monthly, quarterly, semi-annually, or annually. Payments are calculated so that the debt is repaid (amortized) by a specific date. If the periodic payments do not completely amortize the debt by the maturity date, the final payment will be larger than the previous periodic payments. This larger, final payment is known as a "balloon" payment. Term loans sometimes allow early repayment without penalty.

Sometimes personal term loans are available to help finance your initial equity investment in the business. However, this can be risky since the total interest cost on all loans (since none of the money is your own) can be crippling to the company's working capital.

2. Installment financing

Installment financing could be used to finance the purchase of equipment and fixtures where term loans are unavailable. Although some furniture and equipment sales companies may finance this way directly, others will sell to a financing company that, in turn, will do the installment financing. Many supply companies will act as an intermediary between you and the finance company to coordinate the arrangement. In other cases, you may have to shop around to arrange your own installment financing.

Since the assets being financed generally have a life averaging five to ten years, and since the financing agency runs a relatively high risk because of the very low value of second-hand furniture and equipment (and thus its low value as collateral), the length of life of such financing is usually from three to seven years.

There is usually a sizable down payment on such arrangements (from 20 to 30%), and the interest rate is generally much higher than with term loans; it could run as much as five or six points over prime.

Installment loans of this type are generally secured by a chattel mortgage (a lien on the assets financed), which can be registered and which permits the lending company to sell the liened assets if the installment payments are in default.

Alternatively, the lender's security could be by way of a conditional sales contract, which gives the lender title to the assets until you have satisfied all the terms of the contract.

c. LEASING

1. How leasing works

Another method of equipment and fixture financing is leasing. A lease is a contractual arrangement where the asset owner (the lessor) grants you (the lessee) the right to the assets for a specified time in return for periodic rent payments. The leasing of land and/or buildings has long been a method of real property financing in business. Only recently has the popularity of leasing shorter life assets like equipment become fairly common.

Most financial leases are noncancellable and require you to make a series of payments whose total sum will exceed the cost of assets if purchased outright, since the lessor has to make a profit. The lessor is entitled to use depreciation

72

of the assets for tax purposes since the lessor owns the assets.

Maintenance is usually, but not invariably, a cost of the lessor. Generally, also, with a financial lease, the lessor owns any residual value in the assets, although contracts sometimes give the lessee the right to purchase the assets at your option, at a specified price, at the end of the lease period. In some cases, you will have the option to renew the lease for a specified further period.

Some suppliers of equipment will lease directly. In other cases, you will lease from a company that specializes in leasing and has bought the equipment from the supplier. The supplier may act as an intermediary in such cases.

2. Advantages of leasing

Some of the advantages of leasing include flexibility, 100% financing, and tax considerations.

Flexibility is considered to be an advantage because you avoid the risk of obsolescence you might otherwise have if the assets are purchased outright. However, the lessor probably considers the cost of obsolescence when determining the lease rates.

One hundred percent financing of leased assets is possible since there is no down payment required and thus no equity in the asset. One hundred percent lease financing of relatively short-lived assets (such as equipment) also has an advantage even if you have the cash to pay for them outright. This cash is then free for investment in longer-lived assets, such as land or building, that frequently appreciate in value as time goes by. Equipment depreciates very rapidly and usually has little or no residual value.

Finally, income tax is an important consideration. Since lease payments are generally fully tax deductible, there can be an advantage in leasing. On the other hand, ownership permits deduction for income tax purposes of both depreciation and the interest expense on any debt financing of the purchase.

However, what might be advantageous with one lease arrangement may be disadvantageous with another. Each situation must be considered on its own merits as far as tax implications are concerned.

10

WHAT'S INVOLVED IN FINANCING?

Knowing what's involved in securing financing can give you a distinct advantage. The most important fact to remember is that you are in competition with other people and other businesses for the same money. Therefore, being prepared, understanding the procedures involved, and being familiar with the different types of financing available are the first steps in demonstrating good management of a financial proposal.

a. RISK AND INTEREST

In borrowing money, the words risk and interest are closely connected. Risk is the degree of danger the lender has in losing funds loaned to you. Interest is what you pay a lender for the use of borrowed funds. Normally, the higher the risk, the higher the interest rate that will have to be paid. The factors that determine risk include the following:

(a) Your management ability

(b) The amount of your equity in the business

(c) The amount of debt your company already has, if any (i.e., will the company be able to repay all debt obligations?)

(d) The security offered

If your loan proposal is a safe one, it will have relatively little difficulty in finding financing. If the proposal is judged by potential lenders to be risky, there will be more difficulty in finding a lender, the interest rate will probably be high, and the term of the loan (time over which it is to be repaid) will be shorter.

Generally, a franchisee will find more favorable rates of interest and greater amounts of money available if the bank or other lending institute obtains an agreement with the franchisor stating that, if you run into financial difficulties, the franchisor will take whatever action is needed to help correct the situation and ensure that your debt is met. However, an agreement such as that should not be considered by you as an endorsement of the franchisor, or guarantee that the franchise will succeed.

One bank, in checking franchisors, asks the following six simple questions:

(a) Does the franchisor offer a quality product or service? Is there a need for it in the marketplace, and does it enjoy strong customer demand?

(b) What is the franchisor's track record and reputation in the marketplace?

(c) Has the franchisor developed equitable legal agreements, and are they enforceable for the protection of all parties?

(d) Where does the franchisor generate revenue? Is it at the front end from the sale of the franchises, or is it being made over the long term through the distribution of the product or service?

(e) Does the franchisor have the financial stability and resources to back up all obligations to prospective franchisees?

(f) Does the franchisor have any significant financial and/or legal obligation with respect to the franchised location? For example, are the land and building owned, or are they leased? Owning land and/or building presents a stronger case.

You will note that these questions are no different from those (among many) that you were advised (in earlier chapters) to ask about the franchisor.

b. PREPARING THE PAPERWORK
The style and content of a loan application are of major importance when asking for a loan. You should be prepared and confident since you are not just selling an idea but also yourself.

To make the best impression on those approached for funding, it is critical to have all the facts properly documented. Regardless of the type of loan, the information required by the lender will be basically the same.

The lender will want to know who you are, what your plans are, and what these plans will do for the business. The preparation of this information, in answer to the lender's questions, and the analysis that backs it up, is quite simple. The information you would include is discussed below.

1. Resume of the owner(s)

For a planned new business, the lender will want to know something about you (and any other owner or owners), such as education and experience (or lack of it), and how this will be valuable to the business. This information allows the lender to assess the managerial abilities of those who will be running the business. The lender can compare, from past experience in loaning money to other businesses, the relative strengths of your management.

2. Personal financial information

If you do not have a previous business track record the lender will probably need personal financial information about you and the other owner(s). This information will show the lender what further financial support you can fall back on if the business is not immediately successful and requires further owner investment.

3. Financial statements

Financial statement projections will be required, with detailed calculations showing, in particular, how total annual revenue is calculated and what the operating costs are projected to be. If a feasibility study has been prepared, then that feasibility study will serve to provide the lender with full financial projections for as many as five years ahead.

The feasibility study is simply a plan of what is proposed. This financial presentation can be expanded by written explanations detailing each item such as, for example, the size, location and legal description of the land to be purchased, a description of the building, and so forth. Firm items of cost should be specified, as should those that are only estimates.

4. Security offered

The prospective lender will want details of the security offered for any loan. This includes a description of the assets (land, building), when bought, price paid, copies of any mortgages on these assets and the amount (if any) that has been paid toward these mortgages. In particular, if there has been a recent appraisal made on the owned land and building, this will be useful since it will likely indicate that the appraised value of the property is worth more than the price originally paid and the present book value. Photographs of an existing property (that you are buying or leasing) would be useful, as would plans, or even models, if a new building is proposed.

If the land and/or building are not owned, then the lease agreement might form the security offered. In such a case, a copy of the lease agreement should be provided to the lender. A statement from the lessor showing that all rent payments already made (if any) have been made promptly should also be provided.

5. Insurance policies

The lender will want to know if the business is adequately insured against losses and liabilities and, in each case, who the beneficiaries are. Therefore, copies of any insurance policies should be made available to the lender.

6. Presentation

The importance of careful preparation of all the paperwork outlined above can not be overstressed. The professional manner in which this information is prepared and presented to a potential lender will go a long way toward ensuring that the required funds will be obtained.

Accuracy is critical in calculations of revenue and expenses. If careless errors are made in overestimating revenue or underestimating expenses (thus producing a "padded" profit amount), damage will be done to your credibility. The chances of obtaining borrowed funds will be considerably decreased. For this reason, professional help from a financial consultant or an accountant may be necessary.

Even though a suggested list of paperwork items has been outlined above, it might be a good idea to contact potential lenders, in each specific case, to determine what they would like to be presented with. This will ensure that time is not needlessly spent putting together a report that is far more than a lender is interested in or, alternatively, a report that fails to include some specific item that the lender does want.

When seeking financing it is a good idea to make appointments in a businesslike way with each potential lender. That is more likely to portray the image of a professional business operator than just simply walking in the door and asking for money.

c. THE LENDER'S RESPONSE

1. Determine conditions

If a request for financing is approved, find out everything you need to know about the conditions, terms, payment methods, interest rates, security requirements, and any front end charges or fees to be paid.

No commitment to accept the financing should be made until all this information is provided and understood, and its impact on the business analyzed.

If financing is approved, but only if certain other conditions are met, determine if these conditions are severe enough to restrict the operating standards desired. Will the conditions commit you to more than was intended, or are they normal financing requirements that were simply overlooked?

Once a final commitment is arranged, it is a good idea to provide the lender with future copies of financial statements. Frequently this will be one of the requirements for obtaining funding. Even if it is not, it will provide the lender with progress reports about the business and will be helpful to the lender in processing future applications for further financing.

2. Funding denied

If a request for financing is not approved, find out why. Use the lender's experience to advantage. There will be a reason or reasons for not providing financing. Lenders handle many requests for financing and have experience in the financial aspects of many businesses even if they do not have direct management experience.

For example, the lender might be able to see that a proposed new business will run into a shortage of working capital with the financial plan proposed. A shortage of working capital is one of the common reasons for failure of many small, new businesses. If a new business is in trouble because of this, it is often difficult to obtain additional working capital assistance. It is far preferable to ask for additional funds to strengthen working capital at the outset; a potential lender may well be able to point this out as a possible problem with a proposed financing plan.

If there is something else wrong with the financing proposal, see if it can be corrected, and then reapply. If not, use this knowledge when approaching other potential lenders or on future occasions when seeking funds.

d. GOVERNMENT MONEY

1. Small Business Loans Act

If all other sources of funding fail, you might want to consider the Small Businesses Loans Act (SBLA). The SBLA is available to new small business enterprises. For purposes of the act, a small business is one whose annual gross sales are not over $2 million.

Most franchised businesses would be eligible for funding under the SBLA, unless they are engaged in finance, insurance, real estate, and/or a profession, mining, petroleum, natural gas, or for charitable or religious purposes, and as long as the loan is not for working capital requirements or to repay an existing loan.

Loans are available for —

(a) The purchase of fixed or movable equipment, including cost of installation, and the renovation, improvement or modernization of equipment where this is appropriate.

(b) The purchase or construction of new premises or the improvement or modernization of existing premises in which the business is carried on or about to be carried on.

(c) The purchase of land for the operation of a business, including the purchase of a building thereon.

At the present time, the maximum amount that you may borrow under the act at any one time is $100 000. Subject to this maximum, loans can be used to finance up to —

(a) 80% of the cost, including installation, of fixed or movable equipment

(b) 90% of the cost of the purchase or construction of new premises or the purchase of land, or the renovation or improvement of existing premises

The rate of interest on SBLA loans is 1% over the prime lending rates of the chartered banks, and it fluctuates with changes in the prime rate during the term of the loan.

The maximum term of the loan is 10 years. Installments on a loan must be paid at least annually, or more frequently if required by the lender.

All SBLA loans must be secured. Security can take the form of land or chattel mortgages or other security the lender deems necessary. You will also have to sign a note promising to repay the loan. Depending on the circumstances in each case other conditions may be required.

All chartered banks and Alberta Treasury Branches are authorized to make loans under the SBLA. In addition, loans may be made by Credit Unions, Caisses Populaires, or other cooperative societies, trust companies, loan companies, and insurance companies, which have applied and have been designated as lenders under the act. Therefore, if all other sources fail, talk to your own banker or other lender about the SBLA and obtain a credit application. If you want further information about SBLA write to —

Small Businesses Loans Administration
Department of Regional Industrial Expansion
235 Queen Street
Ottawa, Ontario
K1A 0H5

2. Federal Business Development Bank

Finally, you should also be aware of the Federal Business Development Bank, or FBDB. This lender is sometimes referred to as the lender of last resort and was established especially to help those companies that could not obtain financing elsewhere. If your funding application has been turned down by other financial institutions, you may apply to the FBDB. In recent years, they have been particularly helpful to franchisees.

To obtain FBDB financing, the amount of your investment in the business must generally be sufficient to ensure that you are committed to it and that the business may reasonably be expected to be successful.

FBDB financing is available by means of loans, loan guarantees, equity financing, leasing, or by any combination of these methods, in whatever way best suits the particular needs of your business. If loans are involved they are usually at interest rates in line with those of other banks. If equity is involved, the FBDB generally takes a minority interest and is prepared to have you buy back its equity on suitable terms when the business is able to do this.

The FBDB also offers management counselling, management training, and other business information services. If you wish to pursue this, contact your local branch of the FBDB, or write to:

Federal Business Development Bank
P.O. Box 335
Stock Exchange Tower Station
Montreal, Quebec
H4Z 1L4

11

THE FRANCHISE CONTRACT

The backbone of any franchisor/franchisee relationship is the contract or agreement signed by both parties. The franchise agreement differs from the normal contract in that it contains restrictive clauses unique to the franchising relationship. These restrictive clauses limit the franchisee's rights and powers in the conduct of the business.

Sad to say, too many franchisees probably read their copy of the contract with their eyes shut, and even if they do read it with eyes open don't bother checking it out with a lawyer who could explain some of the more complex clauses.

An example of one kind of franchise contract is shown in the Appendix. No two franchise contracts will be alike, so you must carefully read each one you look at.

a. THE CONTRACT IN GENERAL

Do not be talked into making any deposit or down payment to "demonstrate good faith" or "hold a contract open" or "put you at the head of the waiting list" while you study the contract and go over it with your lawyer. Reputable franchisor's don't practise this kind of high pressure salesmanship.

If you do make a deposit with the franchisor because you're sure that you will go ahead, insist that your deposit be held in trust and is so stated in the contract. An honest franchisor will agree to this.

If any promises are made about the franchisor/franchisee relationship that are not in the contract, insist that they be written in before it is signed; if any item is later in dispute the courts generally recognize only what is in the contract.

Don't be afraid to negotiate more favorable terms in the contract if you can. Most ethical franchisors understand that sometimes special conditions are necessary for a particular franchisee, and these may be agreed to as long as the franchisor still gets a return on the investment and maintains integrity in terms of quality control.

However, an ethical franchisor will not negotiate away essential major points that will violate the franchise system. To do so would mean there is no reason to have them in the contract in the first place. If any franchisor is willing to concede such major points, such as erosion of quality standards in order to obtain your fees, this should warn you to turn to other franchisors.

1. Franchisor obligations

There is no such thing as a standard franchise contract. Each contract differs in some way(s) from all others. However, most contracts contain clauses or sections covering the restrictions and obligations of both the franchisor and you, the franchisee. The obligations of the franchisor may include any or all of the following:

(a) Financial assistance

(b) Site selection and layout

(c) Plans and specifications for buildings and other site improvements

(d) Specifications for any necessary equipment and furniture

(e) Promotional and advertising material

(f) Employee hiring assistance

(g) Franchisee and staff training

(h) Business opening assistance

(i) Business operations manuals

(j) A bookkeeping/accounting system

(k) Product supply assurance

(l) Ongoing support in such things as consultation, visits to the premises, and staff retraining

When you have had a chance to review the franchisor's obligations as stated in the contract, try to find out if he or she usually performs the things agreed to in a contract. The best way to do this is to talk to other franchisees. If the franchisor does have a reputation for poor performance, it is better to know this now.

An important consideration in franchisor performance is the closeness of the franchisor's head office, or area supervisor's office, to your location. How far do supervisory personnel have to travel, how many units are they responsible for, and how frequent are visits?

If there are other franchisees in your general area, this can be beneficial to you since it is economically advantageous for the franchisor to service them well. This closeness may provide competition, but it may also have benefits to you in sharing regional advertising campaigns (thus providing all franchisees a higher profile) and reducing purchase and shipping costs.

2. Franchisee obligations

Your obligations as franchisee might include any or all of the following:

- (a) Construction according to plans and specifications provided
- (b) Maintaining construction and opening schedules
- (c) Abiding by lease commitments
- (d) Taking out required insurance
- (e) Undergoing required training
- (f) Provision of adequate working capital
- (g) Devotion of full time effort
- (h) Purchase of products and other items from the franchisor or from an approved supplier
- (i) Agreement to abide by the operations manual
- (j) Proper repair and maintenance of the building and site
- (k) Financial reporting and prompt payment of amounts due
- (l) Proper use of trademark
- (m) Participation in regional or national cooperative advertising

In addition there will probably be clauses involving bankruptcy, transfer of the business, and renewal of the contract, as well as the provisions for fee and royalty payments, trademark usage, facilities design, purchase and sale of the products or services, inventory, pricing, advertising, operating procedures, and accounting methods. Some of these will be discussed in more detail in this chapter.

b. FRANCHISE COSTS

One of the first items mentioned in the contract will be the cost of getting started. This amount can vary from thousands to hundreds of thousands of dollars depending on the type of business involved, who owns what assets, and the services provided by the franchisor.

Although service type franchises (such as income tax services, accounting services, and employment agencies) might charge a franchise fee for the use of their name, operating methods, and forms, this amount is generally relatively nominal. In addition, there may be no ongoing fee or royalty. If there is, for ongoing services such as advertising, it will be a percentage of gross sales or revenue.

In some cases, for example gas stations and some types of retail outlets, there may be no initial fee or continuing percent of revenue. The franchisor leases the station to the franchisee who must purchase supplies from the franchisor (which, along with the rent payments, is where the franchisor makes a profit).

At the other end of the scale is the restaurant or motel franchise where the initial, and ongoing fees, can be quite sizeable depending on who owns the land, building, and equipment and furnishings.

The initial franchise fee generally includes the right to use the trade name, licences, and operating procedures of the franchisor, as well as any initial and ongoing training, and possibly even assistance in site selection. In some rare instances, this initial fee is refundable when the business is on its feet and is making a return on its investment. With some franchisors, there is also a site evaluation fee as an additional charge.

The contract should state when the franchise fee is payable and when it is fully earned. Normally the fee is payable upon signing and is nonrefundable on termination of the agreement for any reason. The contract will usually spell out that the fee is fully earned by the franchisor on the signing of the agreement or, in some situations, when the building plans and specifications have been provided by the franchisor, or when the operations manual has been turned over to you.

In some contracts, the franchisor may require you to put up a certain amount of working capital, in addition to the initial franchise fee, to cover operating costs until the business is making a profit.

c. ROYALTIES

In addition to initial franchise costs, the franchisor is typically paid a royalty. This royalty generally ranges from 2 to 6% of gross sales revenue depending on the services provided. These services might include accounting records, inventory control, management counselling, product research, and, in the case of businesses such as a motel, a referral service. A major item in this royalty cost is the advertising component.

If your participation in advertising campaigns is not tied to a percentage of sales, you should find out what the cost of any advertising done will be, and have this stated in the contract. If you wish to do any local advertising at your own cost, find out if it has to be approved in advance by the franchisor if advertising materials are not provided. Does your advertising royalty have to be paid when sales are not adequate and, if so, what is the sales level that is considered inadequate?

In addition to collecting the royalty payment, the franchisor might also try to increase revenue with interest charges on any financing provided, markups on supplies or equipment you have to buy, or higher than normal rent payments (if the franchisor is also the landlord). The facts in each case should be in the contract.

d. CONSTRUCTION

Where the franchise calls for the franchisee to own the building and/or equipment, the contract may call for a down payment on construction and/or equipment purchase costs.

Where the agreement calls for construction according to the plans and specifications of the franchisor, you should review the contract to see if the franchisor also designates the contractor or if you may choose your own, since, in the latter case, you may save considerably. However, you should have the assurance that the franchisor will give step by step guidance, particularly if the initial fee covers construction supervision.

Review the contract to see if there is a construction performance schedule required. Time is critical in construction, and if your building is held up due to unpredictable labor problems, you may end up in default of contract.

e. LEASED PREMISES

There are a number of different ways in which the premises can be leased if leasing is involved in the franchisor/franchisee contract.

(a) The franchisor may own the land and/or building and lease it to the franchisee.

(b) The franchisee may lease the land and/or building directly from a third party.

(c) The franchisee may own the property, sell it to the franchisor, and lease it back under a "sale leaseback" agreement.

(d) A third party may own the property and lease it to the franchisor, who then subleases it to the franchisee.

If necessary, the contract should clearly spell out who is responsible, you or the franchisor, for negotiating the lease and equipping the premises, including who is to pay what costs.

If a lease is involved, its terms and renewal clauses should be stated and should correspond with the term of the franchise. You wouldn't want a 20-year lease with only a 15-year franchise. Is the price of the lease (if it is held by the franchisor) a reasonable one — or so high as to be a possible hidden cost? Over the life of the lease is there any lease cost escalation clause in the contract?

f. TERRITORY

The contract should be carefully checked for matters such as territorial restrictions and territory exclusivity. Ambiguities are common in this area. The word "exclusive" may imply that the franchisor will not operate, or franchise out to others to operate, a business within the same specified territory.

There is nothing wrong with a nonexclusive territory (in fact it can be advantageous if the market supports it) as long as you know about it in advance and agree to it. Nonexclusivity may provide a reduced sales base, but it can also offer sales benefits by keeping the name of the franchise in front of the public.

In Canada, a franchisor is generally not allowed to keep others from selling his or her products in your territory or shipping goods into your territory from outside it. If the contract states that you have this kind of protection, it is probably illegal. Careful wording is necessary to protect your rights in this area. Your lawyer should check this carefully.

Some questions about territory you might like to ask, and have answers for in the contract, are:

(a) Exactly what are the geographic boundaries of the territory, and is it marked on a map as part of the contract?

(b) Do you have a choice of other territories?

(c) What direct competition is there in the territory chosen, and how many more franchises does the franchisor expect to sell in that area in the next five years? In other words, how much time do you have to build a solid base of customer goodwill?

(d) If the territory is an "exclusive" one, what are the guarantees on this exclusivity?

(e) Even with these guarantees, would you be permitted to open another franchise in the same territory? Alternatively, is the guarantee only valid if you agree to start up one or more franchises within the same territory within a given number of years?

(f) Can your territory be reduced at any time by the franchisor?

(g) Has the franchisor prepared a market survey of the territory? If so, ask for a copy and study it.

(h) Has the specific site within the territory been decided? If not, how will this be done?

g. TRAINING

Most franchise contracts include one or more sections concerning the training provided for a new franchise outlet. Training may involve anywhere from a few hours to several weeks, sometimes at the franchisor's head office. For example, McDonalds operates a Hamburger University at its corporate headquarters and offers a degree in hamburgerology.

The contract should spell out exactly what training is offered and its duration, who pays for it, whether or not transportation and lodging (if involved) are paid by you or the franchisor, and whether or not you, and any other of your staff involved, will be paid a salary or stipend during any extended training period.

In addition, check whether or not the training program includes working in a successful operating unit of the franchise company for a certain period of time.

Some franchise contracts require completion of training as a prerequisite to becoming a franchisee. If your contract has such a provision, determine what the criteria are for successful completion of the training and whether or not your initial franchise fee is refundable should you or any of your employees fail to complete the training satisfactorily.

Since the franchisor/franchisee relationship does not terminate at the end of the training period, the contract should spell out any ongoing on-the-job training that will be offered by company representatives, supervisors, or franchisee coordinators, particularly when new employees are hired. Are any company newsletters, filmstrips, or tapes provided that will keep you and your employees informed about new products or sales methods? If franchisees are expected to attend refresher courses from time to time, is this spelled out, and who pays the costs involved?

h. OPERATIONS

Most franchisors want fairly tight control over your day-to-day operations. This is usually achieved by providing you with a copyrighted operations manual that spells out, procedure by procedure, the ways in which you are expected to run the business. It will include the franchisor's policies and procedures, and cover such details as the hours you must remain open, record-keeping methods, procedures for hiring employees, and, in a restaurant operation, such matters as recipes, portion sizes, food storage and handling procedures, and menu mix and selling prices.

You should inspect the manual if possible prior to signing the franchise agreement to be sure that its requirements are practical as far as you are concerned.

The franchisor's operating policies and procedures are an area that can cause considerable franchisee dissatisfaction once a new business has been successfully established, particularly if they force you to follow inefficient or unprofitable methods, or preclude you from taking advantage of local suppliers' discounted product prices that are lower than the franchisor's. To combat such dissatisfaction, you should carefully read the contract to find out how you must, so to speak, toe the line.

Where you are required to purchase products and/or supplies from the franchisor or approved suppliers (this is referred to as "tied" selling), you should consider the locale of the suppliers since this will dictate shipping costs and distances as well as timing of deliveries, which may be important in the case of perishable supplies. The contract should ensure that you can select the supplier if circumstances permit.

Does the contract call for a minimum purchase quota (a form of hidden cost)? If the contract requires you to purchase only from the franchisor, how are the prices of the products or supplies established? What assurance do you have that the prices will be reasonable or competitive? Does the contract prohibit you from purchasing from other sources where you could buy identical or similar supplies at a lower cost?

Do you have a contracted right to the franchisor's latest innovations or products? Does the contract require any additional fee for this right?

In some contracts, there may be a requirement for you to pay a security deposit to the franchisor for supplies that you order from the franchisor to ensure prompt payment for the goods. These security deposits also protect the franchisor against the goods becoming part of a bankrupt estate or being seized by a landlord for nonpayment of rent under a lease.

i. CONTRACT DURATION, TERMINATION AND RENEWAL

Although some franchisor/franchisee contracts may be as short as a year or so, and some last in perpetuity, the majority run from 10 to 20 years. Where a franchise is tied to a specific location, the term of the franchise contract and the lease agreement, where one exists, should coincide.

During the term of the contract, does it preclude you from engaging in any other form of business? After the contract has expired, are you prohibited from engaging in any similar, competitive business for a stipulated number of years?

Be sure that the term of the contract provides sufficient time for you to amortize your capital payments.

1. Termination

Although, as a franchisee, you might not consider the

termination of a franchise agreement an important consideration because of its relative insignificance at the time you are starting in business, the termination clause is a vitally important part of the contract. This clause deals with how, when, and under what conditions, you may have to give up the business in which you have invested a great deal of time and money.

For example, some franchise contracts provide that at the end of the contract term, or during the contract term, if in the opinion of the franchisor certain conditions have not been met, the franchisor has the absolute privilege of terminating the contract.

If the franchisor terminates under these circumstances, and if the contract does not provide a means whereby a fair market price for the franchise can be established, it may be feasible for the franchisor to repurchase the business at an unfairly low price.

In some cases, franchisors have included a clause in the contract that the repurchase price should not exceed the original franchise fee. This means that after you have **expended considerable effort and funds to build a profitable business you may be faced with having to sell it back to the franchisor at the same price you paid for it years earlier — despite inflation. In other words you will receive no compensation for the goodwill or increased equity you have contributed to the business.**

In particular, you might find that the contract gives the franchisor the right to cancel or fail to renew the contract for some minor reason. Therefore, if the termination clause does appear at the end of a 50-page agreement, look for it and read it diligently.

Some less scrupulous franchisors have been known to use the threat of termination or nonrenewal of contract to force franchisees to accept franchisor policies that are far from the best for the franchisee and may be economically unprofitable. For example, requirements for minimum purchase levels of products that the franchisee must buy from the franchisor or minimum sales quotas that must be achieved may create hardships for the franchisee.

2. Other termination conditions

In any termination clause in the contract, the franchisor may be allowed to repurchase any inventory at a depreciated cost. Also, the agreement will usually provide for the franchisee ceasing all use of the trade names, trademarks, and other identification symbols of the franchisor, and may provide that you cease telephone directory advertising and listings under the franchisor's operating name. You may also be required to return all trademarked and other material to the franchisor and take down all signs bearing the franchisor's name and trademarks.

Even though it is understandable that the franchisor retain the right to cancel, or fail to renew, the contracts of **franchisees who endanger the integrity of all other** franchisees of the system, the termination clauses in many contracts are perceived as giving the franchisor a great deal of power. Unfortunately, in Canada, most provinces have no statutes protecting franchisees against arbitrary or unfair contract termination unless an arbitration clause is in the contract.

Some reputable franchisors have established relationships with their franchisees that allow for an arbitrator to evaluate the franchise so that you will recover not only your initial investment but also a profit from the sale of goodwill you have built up.

Another thing to look at is under what conditions (for example, illness) you can terminate the contract.

Finally, most contracts, while restricting you from any competitive business during the term of the contract, may also restrict you from this for a specified number of years after contract termination, as well as prohibiting you from revealing any trade secrets at any time.

3. Contract renewal

Some contracts contain renewal conditions. Be sure that you understand the renewal provisions of the contract and what the terms, method, and costs of renewal will be.

If the agreement does contain renewal provisions, find out what the renewal fee is, if any. You shouldn't have to pay the initial franchise fees over again. Also, there may be a requirement to repair and upgrade the franchised premises upon renewal, and you should be aware of the costs involved.

If renewal is for leased premises, are the renewal options for both the franchise contract and the lease the same?

j. ASSIGNING OR SELLING

In most contracts, the franchisor has the right to take back an operation upon contract termination as long as there is no renewal clause. In such cases, the franchisor has no obligation to deal with the franchisee further, despite the fact that you, as franchisee, may feel that your many years of hard work to build up the business deserve something better.

If you cannot negotiate some rights to sell the business freely at the end of the contract period, you may well find that you will have to start the contractual process all over again; although this time the price may be much higher, particularly if you have built up a successful business.

Remember that a good franchise opportunity will allow **you to own and build an equity interest in your franchise** which you should be able to sell at any time for whatever value it may have at that time. Check the contract to determine under what conditions you may sell or assign and whether or not the franchisor must approve the new franchisee.

You must understand that the sale or assignment of your business (if possible at a profit to you) is a measure of the freedom or control you have over the value of your enterprise. If you cannot sell it to any one and are subject to rights of first refusal or options to the franchisor on terms very favorable to the franchisor, then this must be taken into account in assessing the investment potential of the business in the first place.

k. BUY BACK

Another problem in many contracts is the franchisor's promise, or lack of it, to buy back a franchise that you cannot operate successfully. Even though the contract may call for the franchisor to buy it back, it is unlikely that the franchisor will assume any of your financial losses.

Beware of a contract that allows the franchisor to buy back the franchise because it is successful, or because the franchisor has sold out to a larger company that wishes to take over the franchisees.

Where buy back of a franchise is permitted by contract, and you agree to it, the agreement should provide for an independent arbitration of the franchise value. If the buy back price only covers the book value of the property, rather than its market value (including any goodwill that you, the franchisee, have built up in making the venture successful), the franchisor may gain handsomely, and you will lose badly.

The franchisor may claim that any goodwill is directly due to the trademark, name, or image, of the franchisor. But what about your own hard work and continued profits if the franchisor were not buying back the franchise? And if the franchise were a losing one, would the franchisor still argue that it is due to the trademark, name, and image? Make sure your lawyer is insistent on this point so that you receive fair value in the event of the buy back of a successful franchise.

l. IN SUMMARY

Many observers of the growth of franchising express concern that franchise contracts generally tend to favor the franchisor, with the franchisee restricted by controls and procedures documented in detail, without the franchisor's responsibilities being equally as well spelled out.

Having your lawyer negotiate the modification of contract clauses before the agreement is signed may ensure better terms. However, once again, beware of franchisors who happily agree to contract changes that may bargain away their quality control standards and integrity. If quality control is bargained away, every franchisee loses, and the franchisor may have gained if the primary objective is to sell franchises rather than establish a successful franchisor/franchisee business.

Finally, before you sign the contract, ask yourself if you are sure that the franchisor can do something you cannot do for yourself. Think carefully about that.

12

SUMMARY AND
FINAL CAUTIONARY COMMENTS

a. SUMMARY

Let me summarize the basic steps you should follow in the process of going into the franchise business. Note that these are only basic steps; for detail, go back and read any relevant chapters.

- Decide on the legal form of organization that you want.

- Select the type of franchise business you would like to go into.

- Visit as many franchised stores as possible that are in that type of business. Talk to the franchisees and their customers to obtain a feel for the acceptance of the system by both the franchisee and the customers.

- Approach various franchisors, or one in particular if you are fairly certain of that franchisor.

- Discuss the situation with the franchisor(s) asking as many questions as possible about the franchise.

- Obtain all documentation and information you can from the franchisor on costs, financial projections, and get a copy of the contract.

- Approach some specific franchisees of that franchisor, and discuss the situation with them.

- If the franchisor does not provide a site location, look for a potential site with enough activity to make the franchise viable.

- If necessary, cost out the land in that area so you are familiar with land prices or land rental costs.

- If it is necessary to construct a building on the site, contact a local contractor (using plans supplied by the franchisor) to have some idea of building costs.

Alternatively, check out local square metre rental costs if a rented building can be used.

• Determine what the equipment, furniture, and fixtures purchase costs will be.

• With all relevant cost information, meet with your banker or other lender to work out the financial debt and equity projections.

• See if the sales and cost projections will provide the required return on your investment and adequate cash flow to repay debt obligations.

• Decision time: use the checklist/worksheet starting on page 103 to help you with your decision. If you feel comfortable, sign the contract (but only after you have thoroughly discussed it with your lawyer), pay your down payment, and proceed. Good luck.

b. CAUTIONARY COMMENTS

Now, here are some final cautionary comments or recommendations, in addition to the many sprinkled throughout this book.

If this is your first business venture, and you are somewhat nervous about going it alone, and particularly about being involved in such matters as site selection, building construction, and similar problems, consider approaching a franchisor who can provide you with a turnkey operation that is well supported by head office backup. You may have to pay more for this, but it will provide you with the security you need until you learn the ropes of running your own small business.

Don't go in on a financial shoestring and a tight time line for getting into business. Delays can occur in such things as negotiating for a site or a lease or in the construction, and if you have loan repayment deadlines to meet, you could be in serious financial trouble before you even begin operations. Have adequate financial backup in case of these potential problems, or illness, or an automobile accident, or other unforeseen problem.

Do not end up being a slave to the business or to the franchisor. You deserve an adequate return on your investment plus a reasonable salary for your time. Make sure the glamour of being in business for yourself does not blinker you to a rational business analysis of your situation. When you realize that you may be working for less than minimum wages with little or no time off, along with a cash investment and total responsibility, it may be time to step back and really assess your personal situation.

Don't enter the franchise business assuming that you can operate with a salaried manager. The business may not be able to support that. If you plan to do so, double check your profit projections. In fact, absentee ownership has led to many problems in the past, and today's franchisors may not permit it since a committed owner/manager is critical to the success of a franchised business.

Beware of franchisors who become rich by selling franchises to under-capitalized franchisees or approving poor locations. You may not be under-capitalized or have a poor location, but indirectly you will suffer through the poor reputation of the franchisor.

Be aware of franchisors who collect kickbacks and commissions from suppliers and keep them instead of passing them on in reduced product costs to you. Know your product costs. The franchisor is entitled to the contracted franchise fee and a royalty, but not to revenue collected and hidden from you.

Be alert to a franchisor who has nothing to lose if you fail. A franchisor who is liable for the rent of your building should you run into difficulty, or has cosigned your loan at the bank, or has some other financial commitment is more likely to want to ensure that you stay in business.

If the franchise requires special equipment available only from the franchisor, be aware that local repair companies may not be readily available in an emergency. In such cases, lack of local repair service could cause you loss of profit.

In the same vein, when you must buy basic products from the supplier, what happens when improper warehousing by the franchisor leaves you short? Similarly, offers at a lower cost may come from a local supplier and it can be frustrating to have to say no and end up eroding your profit base.

Advertising can be a cause for concern if a franchisor exceeds his or her budget and requires you to pay an additional amount in advertising royalties or if the head office advertising agency makes a mistake in running a regional advertisement and your business suffers until head office makes the correction.

Also, there have been conflicts in some franchise systems over the franchisor's use, or non-use, of advertising assessments collected from franchisees. This includes such things as the funds not being used for advertising or being used only in Ontario (where most of the franchisees are), which doesn't help you if you are the only franchisee west of Ontario.

Beware of an unethical practice that has been carried on by more than one franchisor: placing a small advertisement in a large city newspaper and then enlarging it to a full page size as an example of their national newspaper advertising.

You should know if the franchisor controls that you have agreed to live with can be changed if there is a change in top ownership of the franchise system.

If you are planning to enter your first franchised business as a stepping stone to eventual multiple ownership, using the profits from the first to buy the second and so on, be aware that rapid growth in this way can lead to spreading both yourself and your financial resources too thinly. In fact, because of this type of problem, many contracts do not allow more than single unit ownership.

Avoid a franchisor who promises to do your accounting, bank depositing, and debt paying for you, and then send you a cheque for your "profit" each month-end. If you enter into such an agreement, what guarantees do you have that the franchisor will correctly deposit all receipts and diligently pay for all your purchases and other services, as well as make payments on loans and/or mortgages? A franchisor who is dishonest could skim off the top, or even go into bankruptcy, leaving you with no cash but plenty of unpaid bills.

Finally, remember that in the franchisor/franchisee relationship, it is a matter of *caveat emptor* — let the buyer (the franchisee) beware. To reinforce this point, consider the following actual case situation that occurred in Canada recently.

Potential franchisees across Canada were asked to respond to newspaper advertisements offering vending machine distributorships for disposable cigarette lighters. The lighters were from an internationally known manufacturing company and, because of this, seemed to give credibility to the franchisor's scheme. Many franchise purchasers were no doubt influenced by the lighters' household name.

Franchisees were asked to pay about $6 000 for 10 dispensing machines and an initial supply of lighters. Included in the franchise fee was a promise by the franchisor to find suitable "locations" for the vending machines. Purchasers of the franchises were given glossy brochures, prominently displaying the lighter manufacturer's name and logo. Gross potential sales figures were indicated, but no mention was made of expenses involved or of franchisee profits. The lighters cost 60¢ each and were to sell for $1.25.

Unfortunately, this is what happened.

The franchisor's promise to limit the number of machine locations in a particular area was not in writing, and franchisees found competition in their own "exclusive" territory.

Franchisees subsequently discovered that they were responsible for paying municipal and provincial licences and taxes.

Franchisees, without being told this in advance, found out that the franchisor had promised commissions on sales of lighters to some of the owners of the premises in which machines were located. These commissions were payable by the franchisees and not the franchisor!

In other cases, the franchisor promised the owners free advertising on the lighters in return for allowing them to be located on the premises. This "free" advertising was again at the expense of the franchisees.

The "repair" manual for the vending machines turned out to be simply an enlarged picture of the disassembled machine.

Many of the locations of machines turned out to be so poor that only a handful of lighters were sold every month rather than the quantity implied by smooth talking franchise salespersons.

Even though they had paid their franchise fees, some franchisees had to wait months for delivery of their machines. In other cases, the machines did not arrive at all.

Finally, following complaints from franchisees, the lighter company, to protect its own image, cancelled its contract with the franchisor.

*   *   *

Despite this and other horror tales about franchising, you should be confident that under the proper circumstances, many people can, and do, buy and successfully operate a franchise business in Canada.

FRANCHISE CHECKLIST/WORKSHEET

The purpose of this checklist/worksheet is to aid you in your follow through of starting out a franchised business. This checklist contains most of the key questions that relate to the typical franchise. However, in some situations, questions will not be relevant and may be omitted. In other cases, questions other than those listed may need to be asked. In other words, this checklist/worksheet is a guide.

For more detail, refer to the relevant chapters in this book to determine why particular questions need to be asked. If you plan to follow through with a number of different franchisors it might be a good idea to duplicate some additional sets of blank checklist/worksheets before you fill in any of the spaces.

a. PREAMBLE

1. Have you taken a self-assessment of your skills, strengths, and weaknesses to try to determine whether or not you should be going into business for yourself?

     _____ yes

     _____ no (The answer to this question should be yes, otherwise you may be misleading yourself.)

2. What form of business organization have you decided on (see chapter 3)?

     _____ Proprietorship

     _____ Partnership

     _____ Incorporated company

3. What kinds or types of franchised business are you interested in, in order of priority (see chapter 2)?

     1. _____

2. _____

3. _____

4. How do you plan to operate the business, given a choice (see chapter 4)?
   _____ Licensee
   _____ Dealer
   _____ Distributor
   _____ Business format

b. FRANCHISOR/FRANCHISEES (see chapter 5)

1. Franchisor name _____

2. Franchisor address _____

   _____

3. Is the franchisor a
   _____ Proprietorship
   _____ Partnership
   _____ Incorporated company

4. If incorporated, is the company
   _____ Public
   _____ Private

5. If private who is the banker? _____

6. Who are some of the major suppliers?

   _____

   _____

   _____

7. Are audited financial statements of the company available? _____ yes _____ no

8. What are the names of some of the principals involved?

_____

_____

_____

9. How long has the company been in business?
   _____ years

10. When was its first franchise issued? _____

11. How many franchisees are there? _____

12. Are these franchisees generally
   _____ Local
   _____ Regional
   _____ National
   _____ International

13. Where are three franchises located that you can readily visit?

Owner	Address	Telephone	Date Started

   (See the list of questions to ask these franchisees in the section headed "Other franchisees" in chapter 5.)

14. Of all sales outlets how many are
   _____ Franchisee operated
   _____ Company (franchisor) operated

15. Have any of the company operated franchises been recently taken back by the franchisor?

_____ yes _____ no. If yes, why?

_____

_____

16. How many additional franchises are to be sold in the next year or two _____ and in the next two to five years? _____

17. Have any franchisees failed in the past two years?

_____ yes _____ no.
If yes, which ones were they?

_____

_____

_____

18. What is the franchisor's explanation for any failures?

_____

_____

19. What is the franchisees' explanation for any failures?

_____

_____

20. What is the Better Business Bureau, or any other third party's, explanation for any failures?

_____

_____

21. If there is an inspection system how frequent is it

    _____ and what does the franchisor look for?

    _____

    _____

22. Is there a franchisee advisory council?

    _____ yes _____ no

23. Is this a pyramiding form of franchising?

    _____ yes _____ no. (See chapter 6.)

c. THE PRODUCT (see chapter 5)

1. Is the main product manufactured by

    _____ the franchisor or

    _____ a third party

2. Does the product have

    _____ a long-term demand

    _____ a seasonal demand

    _____ a fad demand

    _____ limited appeal (for example, to a specific age group)

    _____ a growing market (particularly in your area)

3. Is the product

	yes	no
Price competitive	___	___
Worth the price	___	___
Satisfactory to you as a prospective purchaser	___	___
Reputable	___	___
Safe	___	___

Protected   ____   ____
Guaranteed   ____   ____

4. Does the franchisor establish the main product(s) prices?

    _____ yes _____ no

5. Do you have to carry specific franchisor products?

    _____ yes _____ no

6. Are minimum order quantities required?

    _____ yes _____ no

7. What product payment terms are required?

    _____

    _____

8. Are there any government standards and regulations required?

    _____ yes _____ no
If yes does the product meet those requirements?
    _____ yes _____ no

9. Who provides guarantees/warranties and at what cost?

    _____

10. Who pays for repairs? _____

11. Is a well known personality associated with the product?

    _____ yes _____ no
If yes, is this
      _____ a token representation or
      _____ an investment in time and effort by that personality?

12. Does the product or service require
    _____ a specific sales method or
    _____ a combination of sales methods

13. What products or services does the franchisor plan to add in the next year or two _____

    _____

    and in the next two to five years? _____

    _____

14. Has the franchisor made an effort to keep products in line with the times?
    _____ yes _____ no

15. Are you obligated to sell new products introduced by the franchisor?
    _____ yes _____ no

16. Can you sell products or services other than those from the franchisor?
    _____ yes _____ no

d. FEES AND ROYALTIES (see chapters 6 and 11)

1. How much is the initial franchise fee? _____
   When is initial franchise fee to be paid? _____

2. Exactly what does it include (for example, startup inventory, equipment and fixtures)?

   _____

   _____

   _____

3. Who pays for:

	Franchisor	Franchisee
Legal fees	_____	_____
Permits/licences	_____	_____
Insurance	_____	_____

4. Under what circumstances, if any, is the initial franchise fee refundable?

_____

5. Does the franchisor require you to put up a certain amount of working capital in addition to the franchise fee? _____ yes _____ no. If yes, how much? _____

6. What ongoing advertising and/or royalty fees are there and how are they calculated?

_____

7. Exactly what does the franchisor offer for these ongoing fees?

_____

_____

8. What are the advertising media used?
   _____ Radio   _____ TV
   _____ Newspaper   _____ Magazine
   _____ Direct mail   _____ Other

9. Are any examples of print advertising material available?

   _____ yes _____ no

10. When do these ongoing advertising (royalty) fees have to be paid?

_____

11. Do these ongoing fees include all advertising?

_____ yes _____ no

12. Do you still have to pay the advertising fee or royalty if your sales are not up to forecast?

_____ yes _____ no

13. May you do your own local advertising?

_____ yes _____ no

If yes, what support will the franchisor provide, particularly with opening day costs?

_____

14. Does local advertising have to be approved in advance by the franchisor?

_____ yes _____ no

e. BUILDING AND EQUIPMENT (see chapter 6)

1. What building standards are required?

_____

_____

2. Can an existing building be converted?

_____ yes _____ no

3. Who pays for this? _____

4. What layout design restrictions are there?

_____

_____

5. If a new building is required does the franchisor handle construction?

_____ yes _____ no

6. Can you choose your own contractor?

_____ yes _____ no

7. Is a construction performance schedule required?

_____ yes _____ no

8. Must specific equipment and fixtures be used?

_____ yes _____ no

If yes, must you buy these from the franchisor _____ or can you shop around? _____

9. If you must buy equipment and fixtures from the franchisor, what are the purchase terms and conditions?

_____

10. Are there requirements for building maintenance and repair?

_____ yes _____ no

If yes, how frequently must this be done _____ and at whose cost? _____

11. In leased premises, are you _____ or the franchisor _____ responsible for negotiating the lease?

12. Does the lease term correspond with the franchise term?

_____ yes _____ no

f. TRAINING (see chapters 6 and 11)

1. Exactly what training is offered?

_____

_____

_____

2. How long is it? _____

3. Is there any cost to you? _____ yes _____ no

4. Who pays for travel and accommodation costs?

   _____

5. Is a salary or stipend paid during this training period?
   _____ yes _____ no

6. Does training include working in a successful franchise outlet?
   _____ yes _____ no

7. If the contract requires successful completion of training, what are the criteria for successful completion, and under what circumstances might the initial franchise fee be refundable if training is not completed?

   _____

   _____

   _____

   _____

8. What provision is there for ongoing training in such cases as:
   a. Employee turnover

   _____

   _____

b. Introduction of new products

_____

_____

What cost is involved, if any? _____

g. **FRANCHISOR CONTROLS** (see chapter 6)
What specific franchisor controls are included?

_____

_____ _____

_____

_____

_____

_____

h. **SALES AND EXPENSE DATA** (see chapter 6)
1. Are sales and expense forecasts available?
   _____ yes _____ no
   If yes are they for a
   _____ Franchised operation
   _____ Franchisor operated outlet

2. If for a franchised operation, where exactly is it located?

   _____

3. Are sales figure projections attainable in your location?
   _____ yes _____ no

4. What expense figures might change for your location?

_____

_____

_____

5. Are some expenses included, or excluded, from the statement presented that you might, or might not, have?

_____ yes _____ no

If yes, which ones might they be?

_____

_____

_____

i. LOCATION (see chapter 7)

1. Who selects the location?

_____

2. If a site location specialist is required, who pays this cost?

_____

3. If a site has already been selected, do you feel it is the right one (consider, for example, the socio-economic factors)?

_____ yes _____ no

4. Where important, is the site

	yes	no
a. Visible	_____	_____
b. Accessible	_____	_____
c. Suitable	_____	_____

5. Have the following bylaws/zoning factors been checked out:

	yes	no
a. Building codes	_____	_____
b. Fire regulations	_____	_____
c. Sign ordinances	_____	_____
d. Sewers	_____	_____
e. Water mains	_____	_____
f. Power supplies	_____	_____
g. Other utilities	_____	_____
h. Highways	_____	_____
i. Land deed for easements/ restrictions	_____	_____

6. Would the site be suitable for future expansion?

_____ yes _____ no

j. FINANCIAL (see chapters 8, 9, and 10)

1. Summary of initial costs involved (insert relevant figures):

Land	$ _____
Building	_____
Equipment/fixtures	_____
Feasibility study cost	_____
Design work	_____
Working capital	_____
Franchise fees	_____
Legal/accounting	_____
Other	_____
Total investment required	$ _____

2. Summary of sources of financing total investment required:

Amount

Debt
Source 1 _____ $ _____
Source 2 _____ _____
Source 3 _____ _____

Equity
Source 1 _____ _____
Source 2 _____ _____
Source 3 _____ _____

Total $_____

3. What will be your return on investment? _____

4. How does that compare with leaving your money in the bank?

_____

5. Will the cash flow from the business be sufficient to:
  a. Carry you until the business is well established? _____ yes _____ no
  b. Pay off any debts you incur to get into business? _____ yes _____ no

k. TERRITORY (see chapter 11)

1. Has there been a franchise in this area already?
  _____ yes _____ no
  If yes, is it still in business?
  _____ yes _____ no
  If not, why not?

_____

_____

(Since territory rights are such a critical matter, you are specifically referred to this section of chapter 11 where comments and a list of possible questions that you may pose to the franchisor is detailed.)

l. OPERATIONS (see chapter 11)

1. Is there a copyrighted operations manual?

   _____ yes _____ no

   If yes, when do you obtain a copy? _____

2. Are all aspects of this manual acceptable to you?

   _____ yes _____ no

   If no, list those items that you would like to discuss with the franchisor.

   _____

   _____

   _____

   _____

   _____

3. Do you have a contracted right to the franchisor's latest innovations or products?

   _____ yes _____ no

   If yes, does the contract require an additional fee for this? _____ yes _____ no

4. Does head office support include:

	yes	no
Accounting and finance	_____	_____
Advertising/promotion	_____	_____
Manufacturing	_____	_____
Marketing/sales	_____	_____
Personnel	_____	_____

Purchasing _____ _____
Research/development _____ _____

5. Is there a field person assigned to your territory?
   _____ yes _____ no
   If yes, what is his or her name? _____
   How many other franchises does he or she have
   responsibility for? _____

m. CONTRACT DURATION, TERMINATION, AND RENEWAL (see chapter 11)

1. Does the contract have a termination clause?
   _____ yes _____ no
   If yes, (which it should have), have you carefully read
   it? _____ yes _____ no

2. Does the termination clause allow the franchisor to
   buy back the franchise prior to termination?
   _____ yes _____ no

3. Does the termination clause include provision for fair
   compensation for the franchisor's purchase of
   inventory? _____ yes _____ no;
   fixtures and equipment? _____ yes _____ no;
   and goodwill? _____ yes _____ no

4. If there is disagreement about the prices to be paid on
   termination, is there provision for an arbitrator?
   _____ yes _____ no

5. Under what conditions can the franchisor terminate
   the contract?

   _____

   _____

   _____

6.   Under what conditions can you terminate the contract?

_____

_____

_____

7.   In the event of contract termination (either before expiry or not), what restrictions are there on you once again going into business for yourself?

_____

_____

8.   What renewal provisions (methods, and costs) are in effect at the end of the contract term?

_____

_____

_____

9.   Under what conditions may you sell or assign the contract, if you desire, prior to its termination?

_____

_____

_____

10. Is there provision in the contract for the franchisor to buy the business back if it is not successful?

_____ yes _____ no

If yes, under what conditions?

_____

n. THREE FINAL CRITICAL QUESTIONS

1. Are there any important facts that you have made note of on this worksheet that are not in writing in the contract?

   _____ yes _____ no

   If yes, which ones:

   _____

   _____

   _____

   _____

   _____

2. Has your lawyer read the contract and advised you?

   _____ yes _____ no

3. Can the franchisor do something for you that you cannot do for yourself?

   _____ yes _____ no

APPENDIX
SAMPLE FRANCHISE CONTRACT

THIS AGREEMENT made the _____ day of _____ 198___.

BETWEEN:

<u>THE SANDWICH TREE RESTAURANTS CORPORATION</u>, a Company, duly incorporated under the laws of British Columbia, and having an office at Suite 120 - 535 West 10th Avenue, in the City of Vancouver, in the Province of British Columbia, V5Z 1K9

(hereinafter called "the Company")

OF THE FIRST PART

AND:

(hereinafter called "the Franchisee")

OF THE SECOND PART

AND:

(hereinafter called "the Guarantor")

OF THE THIRD PART

<u>WHEREAS</u>:

A.   The Company is engaged in the business of franchising limited menu, self-service restaurants, and, in connection therewith, licencing the use of service marks and trademarks, which said restaurants are herein sometimes referred to as THE SANDWICH TREE, and

B.   The Company has established a high reputation with the public as to the quality of products and services available at THE SANDWICH TREE, which has been and continues to be a unique benefit to the Company and its Franchise Programme; and

*This sample contract is included courtesy of The Sandwich Tree Restaurants Corporation. Note that this type of contract is fair and reasonable to both parties.

C.   The Franchisee recognizes the benefits to be derived from being identified with and licensed by the Company and being able to utilize the system, names and marks which the Company makes available to its Franchisees; and

D.   The Franchisee desires to be franchised to operate a SANDWICH TREE RESTAURANT pursuant to the provisions hereof and at the location specified herein, and the Franchisee has had a full and adequate opportunity to be thoroughly advised of the terms and conditions of this Franchise Agreement by counsel of its own choosing.

NOW THEREFORE, in consideration of the mutual covenants herein contained, the parties agree as follows:

1.   <u>FRANCHISE PAYMENT</u>. The Company acknowledges payment to it by the Franchisee of the sum as set out in Rider 1, for initial and continuing assistance essential to the Franchisee consisting of the training and the services detailed in clauses 2(b), 2(c) and 2(d). The Franchisee acknowledges that the grant of the franchise constitutes the sole consideration for the payment of the Franchise fee and that sum shall be fully earned by the Company upon execution and delivery of this Agreement. No further franchise fee shall be payable during the term herein granted or any renewal thereof. In the event any security or other evidence of indebtedness is accepted by the Company as partial payment, then the prompt and faithful discharge of such obligation shall be a material consideration. Failure of the Franchisee to pay such obligation on its due date shall constitute a default of this Agreement and the Company shall not be obliged to give notice of such default, anything in Clause 27(f) to the contrary notwithstanding.

2.   <u>SERVICES BY THE COMPANY</u>. The Company agrees during the term of this Agreement to use its best efforts to maintain the high reputation of THE SANDWICH TREE and in connection therewith to make available to the Franchisee:

(a)   Initial standard specifications and plans for the location, equipment, furnishings, decor, layout and signs identified with SANDWICH TREE RESTAURANTS, together with advice and consultation concerning them.

(b)   A pre-opening training programme conducted at the Company's training centre and at a Franchised Restaurant.

(c)   Opening supervision and assistance from employees of the Company at the Franchisee's premises.

(d)   Opening and ongoing promotion programmes conducted under the direction of the Company's Marketing Department.

(e)   The Company's confidential standard business policies and operations data instruction manuals (hereinafter collectively called "the Manual") a copy of which will be delivered and loaned to the Franchisee for the term hereof.

(f)   Such merchandising, marketing, and advertising research data and advice as may be from time to time developed by the Company and deemed by it to be helpful in the operation of THE SANDWICH TREE RESTAURANTS.

(g)   Consultation and advice by the Company's field supervisors, either by personal visit, telephone, mail or otherwise, as may from time to time be reasonably required by the Franchisee.

(h)   Such special recipe techniques, food preparation instructions, new restaurant services and other operational developments as may be from time to time developed by the Company and deemed by it to be helpful in the operation of a SANDWICH TREE RESTAURANT.

(i)   A standardized accounting, cost control and portion control system.

(j)   The Company management representative agrees to spend three weeks from date of opening in the Franchised Restaurant assisting in all facts of its operation.

3.   DEFAULT. If the Company fails to perform any of the obligations set out in clauses 2(a) to 2(j) inclusive, it shall be deemed to be in default under this Agreement.

4.   FRANCHISE GRANT. Subject to the terms and conditions of this Agreement, and the continuing good faith performance thereof by the Franchisee, the Company grants to the Franchisee the franchise to operate a SANDWICH TREE RESTAURANT at the location of the premises as set out in Rider 2 (the "premises"); and in consideration of the payment by the Franchisee of the royalties and advertising and sales promotion contribution hereinafter specified, the Company licences to the Franchisee for the term hereof the Company's right to use at the premises and in the operation of such restaurant, the name THE SANDWICH TREE, together with such other insignia, symbols and trademarks which may be approved and authorized by the Company from time to time in connection with SANDWICH TREE RESTAURANTS, and the good will derived from such previous use by the Company.

5.   AREA. This franchise shall be exclusive within the area set out in Rider 3.

6.   TERM. The term of this Franchise Agreement shall commence on the date the Franchisee's restaurant opens for business and shall expire at midnight on the date preceding the anniversary date of said opening as set out in Rider 4, unless sooner terminated in accordance with the terms and conditions hereof.

7.   PREMISES. The Franchisee shall conduct business from the premises only if and when the premises have been improved, decorated, furnished and equipped with restaurant equipment, furnishings and supplies which meet the Company's specifications. The restaurant design and leasehold improvements will be in strict conformity with plans and specifications prepared by the Company's architects.   During the term of this agreement, the premises shall be used only by the Franchisee and solely for the purpose of operating a SANDWICH TREE RESTAURANT pursuant to the terms of this Agreement.

8.   TRAINING. The Franchisee will designate a person approved by the Company as a trainee to attend the Company's training centre. The Company approval of the trainee shall be based upon results of reasonable testing procedures. All expenses of travel, room, board and wages of trainee shall be paid by the Franchisee. A portion of trainee's schooling will consist of in-store training at a training centre approved by the Company. If at any time, the trainee shall voluntarily withdraw from training, or shall be unable to complete training, or shall fail to demonstrate to the satisfaction of the Company, an aptitude, spirit or ability to comprehend and carry out the course of study, methods, and procedures being taught, then in such event, the Company shall have the right to require the Franchisee to appoint another trainee to undertake and successfully complete the training course.

9.   ROYALTIES. The Franchisee agrees in consideration of the Company licencing its use of the name SANDWICH TREE, together with such other trademarks and service marks as may be authorized for use by the Company, and in consideration of the covenants and promises of the

SAMPLE FRANCHISE CONTRACT — Continued

Company herein and representations made by the Company inducing the
Franchisee to enter into this Agreement to pay a monthly royalty in the
amount as set out in Rider 5 of the Franchisee's gross sales. Royalties
shall be paid on or before the tenth (10th) day of each month and shall
be based upon sales for the preceding calendar month.

10.   ADVERTISING AND SALES PROMOTION. The Franchisee agrees, as
partial consideration for the grant of this Franchise, to pay to the
Company a monthly advertising and sales promotion contribution. This sum
shall be equal to that per cent of the Franchisee's gross sales as set
out in Rider 6. The Advertising and sales promotion contribution shall
be paid on or before the tenth (10th) day of each month and shall be based
upon the Franchisee's gross sales for the preceding calendar month.
The advertising and sales promotion contribution shall be expended by
the Company at its discretion for advertising and sales promotion both
in the Franchisee's market area and on a regional basis, except for that
portion used for creative and production cost of advertising and sales
promotion elements, and for those market research expenditures which are
directly related to the development and evaluation of the effectiveness
of advertising and sales promotion.

11.   GROSS SALES. The term "gross sales" as used in this agreement,
shall include the sale of all goods, wares, merchandise, food, non-alcoholic
beverages, or services; provided however, that income from cigarette
vending machines and delivery service charges shall be excluded in
determining gross sales. The term "gross sales" shall exclude the sale
of alcoholic beverages and the amount of any federal, provincial or
municipal sales tax, or other similar taxes which may now or hereafter
be imposed upon or be required to be paid by the Franchisee as against
its sales and it shall also exclude cash received as payment in credit
transactions where the extension of credit itself has already been
included in the figure upon which the royalty and maximum advertising
cost percentage is computed.

12.   ACCOUNTING. The Franchisee agrees to keep complete records of
its business. The Franchisee shall furnish monthly profit and loss
statements for the preceding month and a profit and loss statement for
each fiscal year to the end of the preceding month. The Franchisee shall
also submit to the Company quarterly balance sheets, the first of which
shall be for the period ending three (3) months after the beginning of
the Franchisee's first fiscal year. All profit and loss statements and
balance sheets shall be in accordance with the system of accounting as
contained in the Manual, and shall be submitted to the Company not later
than the fifteenth (15th) day of the month following the period for which
the written statements shall be submitted. At the request of the
Franchisee, the Company shall render accounting services to the Franchisee
providing a monthly profit and loss statement, and a monthly balance sheet
for a monthly fee as set out in Rider 7.

13.   CERTIFIED STATEMENTS. The Franchisee shall submit an annual
financial statement as to gross sales, which statement shall be certified
correct by a certified chartered accountant within ninety (90) days after
the close of its fiscal year. If the Franchisee wishes to apply for an
additional Franchise, or if the Franchisee applies to the Company for
financial assistance or relief, or seeks a financial arrangement with the
Company that differs substantially from existing Company policies, then, in
any such event, the Franchisee shall be required to submit a complete
financial statement which shall be certified to by a certified chartered
accountant.

14.   AUDITS. The Franchisee agrees that the Company, or its
agents, shall, at the Company's expense, at all reasonable times, and so
as not to interfere with the Franchisee's operations, have the right to
examine or audit the books and accounts of the Franchisee to verify the
gross sales as reported by the Franchisee.

15.   STANDARDS AND UNIFORMITY OF OPERATION. The Franchisee agrees
that the Company's special standardized design and decor of SANDWICH TREE
RESTAURANT and uniformity of equipment and layout, and adherence to the
Manual are essential to the image of a SANDWICH TREE RESTAURANT. In
recognition of the mutual benefits accruing from maintaining uniformity of
appearance, service, products and marketing procedures, it is mutually
covenanted and agreed:

(a)   Premises. Except as specifically authorized by the
Company, the Franchisee shall not alter the appearance of the
improvements or the premises. The Franchisee will promptly make
all repairs and alterations to the restaurant and to the premises
as may be determined by the Company to be reasonably necessary.
The Franchisee will paint its restaurant when the Company, in the
exercise of reasonable discretion, determines it advisable, and paint
colours will be in accordance with specifications of the Company.
The Company shall not ask for a colour change if painting is not otherwise required.

(b)   Signs. The Franchisee agrees to display the Company's
names and trademarks at the premises, in the manner authorized by
the Company. The Franchisee agrees to maintain and display signs
reflecting the current image of the Company. The colour, size, design,
and location of said signs shall be as specified by the Company. The
Franchisee shall not place or permit to be placed additional signs or
posters on the premises without the written consent of the Company.

(c)   Equipment. The Franchisee shall acquire through the
Company or other Company approved sources by purchase or lease,
machinery, equipment, furnishings, signs and other personal property
(hereinafter collectively called "equipment"). Appended hereto as
Appendix "A" is a list of equipment which must be used by the Franchisee
in the operation of its business. The Franchisee agrees to maintain
such equipment in excellent working condition. As items of equipment
become obsolete, or mechanically impaired to the extent that they
require replacement, the Franchisee will replace such items with either
the same or substantially the same type and kinds of equipment as are
being installed in a SANDWICH TREE RESTAURANT at the time replacement
becomes necessary. All equipment used in SANDWICH TREE RESTAURANTS,
whether purchased from the Company or other approved suppliers pursuant
to clause 15 (d), 15 (e), and 15 (h), shall meet the Company's
specification.

(d)   Vending Machines, etc. Telephones, newspaper racks, juke
boxes, gum machines, games, rides or any coin vending machines shall
not be installed on the premises without the written approval of the
Company. The Company shall not object to the installation of a single
cigarette vending machine and a coin telephone which meet the Company
specifications, including their location on the premises.

(e)   Menu. The Franchisee agrees to serve only the menu items
specified by the Company, to follow all specifications and formulas of
the Company as to contents and weight of unit products served, and to
sell no other food or drink item or any other merchandise of any kind
without the prior written approval of the Company. The Franchisee agrees
that all food and drink items will be served in containers bearing
accurate reproductions of the Company's service marks and trademarks
unless otherwise authorized by the Company. Such imprinted items shall
be purchased by the Franchisee through the Company or through a supplier
or manufacturer approved in writing by the Company. The Company agrees
to assist the Franchisee in establishing approved sources of supply of
meat, bakery and all other food items and their containers.

(f)   Standards. The Franchisee agrees that it will operate
its restaurant in accordance with the standards, specifications and
procedures set forth in the Manual. The Franchisee agrees further
that changes in such standards, specifications and procedures may
become necessary from time to time and agrees to accept as reasonable
such modifications, revisions and additions to the Manual which the
Company, in the good faith exercise of its judgment, believes to be

127

necessary. The Franchisee agrees not to deviate from the standards of cleanliness and sanitation as set and maintained by the Company in the operation of a SANDWICH TREE RESTAURANT. It is understood and agreed that curb service is not approved by the Company.

(g)   Hours of business. The Franchisee shall operate its business on the premises continuously from the date on which the Franchise Restaurant opens for business during normal business hours during the day and at such hours each evening as may be determined by the Company. The Franchisee may remain open for business from 7:00 a.m. to 11:00 p.m. daily unless the Company consents to other hours or days at the request of the Franchisee. The Company recognizes that considerations peculiar to the location of the premises may make it desirable to alter the hours of operation, and the Company will not unreasonably withhold its consent to modify such hours.

(h)   Alternate Suppliers. Irrespective of any other provision hereof, if the Franchisee gives the Company notice sufficiently in advance to permit supplier verification and specification testing, that it wishes to purchase equipment, food, suppliers, or containers from reputable, dependable sources other than the Company or its designated or previously approved sources of supply, the Company will not unreasonably withhold the prompt approval of such purchases provided such purchases conform to the appearance, quality, size or portion (and, where applicable, taste), and uniformity standards and other specifications of the Company. The Company may require that samples of comestibles from alternate suppliers be delivered to the Company or to a designated independent testing laboratory for testing before approval and use. A charge not to exceed the actual cost of the test may be made to the Franchisee by the Company or by an independent testing laboratory designated by the Company.

(i)   Right of Entry and Inspection. The Company, or its authorized agent and representative shall have the right to enter and inspect the premises and examine and test food products and supplies for the purpose of ascertaining that the Franchisee is operating the SANDWICH TREE RESTAURANT in accordance with the terms of this Agreement and the Manual. Inspection shall be conducted during normal business hours. The Company shall notify the Franchisee of any deficiencies detected during inspection and the Franchisee shall promptly and diligently correct any such deficiencies. Upon written notice by the Company that any equipment, food, supplies or imprinted containers do not meet the specifications, standards and requirements of the Company, the Franchisee shall immediately desist and refrain from the further use thereof.

.16.   The Franchisee agrees to secure and pay premiums thereon for the term and any renewal of this Agreement, a Comprehensive General Liability Policy to a limit of no less than $1,000,000.00 and including the following extensions of coverage: Non-Owned Automobile, Employees as Additional Insureds, Personal Injury, Products and Completed Operations, Contingent Employer's Liability, Blanket Contractual, Broad Form Property Damage, Occurrence Property Damage, Voluntary Medical Payments, Employer's Liability. The Franchisee agrees to name the Company in the policy as an additional insured and such policy shall stipulate that the Company shall receive thirty (30) days' written notice of cancellation. The Franchisee further agrees to insure the following:

(a)   Fixtures and tenant's improvements to their full replacement value, as set out in Rider 8.

(b)   Tenant's Fire Legal Liability, to the full replacement value of the occupied premises, as set out in Rider 9.

(c)   Stock to its full replacement value, as set out in Rider 10.

Copies of all insurance policies shall be furnished promptly to the company, together with proof of payment thereof. All policies shall be renewed and evidence of renewal mailed to the Company prior to any expiration date.

17.   INDEMNIFICATION. The Franchisee is responsible for all loss or damage and contractual liabilities to third persons originating or in connection with the operation of the SANDWICH TREE RESTAURANT, operated by the Franchisee, and for all claims or demands for damages to property or for injury, illness or death of persons directly or indirectly resulting therefrom; and the Franchisee agrees to defend, indemnify and save the Company harmless of, from and with respect to any such claims, loss or damage.

18.   TAXES. The Franchisee shall promptly pay when due all taxes and licence fees levied or assessed by reason of its operation and performance under this Agreement. The Franchisee further agrees to secure and pay premiums to the Worker's Compensation Board covering all its employees and, if applicable, to pay federal unemployment deductions, provincial sales tax, (including any sales or use tax on equipment purchased or leased), and all other taxes and expenses of operating the SANDWICH TREE RESTAURANT on the premises. In the event of any bona fide dispute as to the liability for the taxes assessed against the Franchisee, the Franchisee may contest the validity or the amount of the tax in accordance with procedures of the taxing authority. In no event, however, shall the Franchisee permit a tax sale or seizure by levy of execution or similar writ or warrant to occur against the premises or equipment.

19.   OPTION TO RENEW. If the Franchisee shall have complied with all of the terms and conditions of this Agreement and any other agreement between the Franchisee and the Company, and shall have complied with the operating standards and criteria established for the SANDWICH TREE RESTAURANTS, then, at the expiration of the term hereof, the Company will offer the Franchisee the opportunity to remain a Franchisee for a further period as set out in Rider 11 provided that:

(a)   The Franchisee shall agree to make such capital expenditures as may be reasonably required to renovate and modernize the premises, signs and equipment so as to reflect the then current image of the SANDWICH TREE RESTAURANT.

(b)   The Franchisee must have the right to remain in possession of the premises, or other premises acceptable to the Company, for the new term. If the Franchisee elects (or is required) to relocate, then the Franchisee shall pay the Company's reasonable legal costs in connection with such relocation. The Company shall not be required to extend its credit or resources in obtaining financing for premises or equipment.

(c)   If the Company, or its affiliate is the Lessee of the premises, and the Franchisee so requests, the Company shall use its best efforts to renew the Lease upon the term and conditions for renewal therein contained, and the Franchisee shall have the right to remain in the premises for the term of the renewal upon it assuming in writing all of the Company's obligations under the Lease during the renewal term.

(d)   The Franchisee shall execute a new Franchise agreement in substantially the same form as this Agreement differing only as to royalty fees, advertising contributions and amounts of insurance coverage.

(e)   The Franchisee shall not pay the then current Franchise fee as established by the Company, but it shall reimburse the Company for the cost and other expenses incurred incident to the exercise of the Franchisee's option.

(f)   The Franchisee shall give the Company written notice of its desire to exercise its option to continue as a Franchisee not less than fifteen (15) months prior to the expiration of the term of this Agreement.

20.   SHAREHOLDERS. The shareholders of the Franchisee are those individuals as set out in Rider 12, whose shares shall be closely held.

21.   GUARANTOR'S INTEREST. The Guarantor is and shall continue to be the legal and beneficial owner of at least fifty-one (51%) per cent of the issued shares of the Franchisee, and shall act as the Franchisee's principal officer. Provided the Guarantor retains controlling interest of the Franchisee, he may sell, transfer or assign shares in the Franchisee to members of his immediate family or to a trustee for same.

22.   CORPORATE ALTERATIONS BY FRANCHISEE. The Franchisee shall not, except with the written consent of the Company (such consent not to be unreasonably withheld):

       (a) Issue any additional shares in its capital stock;

       (b) Make any alterations in its capital structure;

       (c) Commence proceedings for its winding up, re-organization or dissolution;

       (d) Permit the transfer of any of its shares except if otherwise permitted by this Agreement.

       (e) Sell, transfer, assign, mortgage, pledge, charge or otherwise encumber the whole or substantially the whole of its undertaking or its property or its rights, or consolidate or combine with any other corporation;

       (f) Increase the number of its directors;

       (g) Amend, repeal, or vary any provisions contained in its memorandum or articles, except for the purposes of giving effect to this Agreement.

23.   ARTICLES OF FRANCHISEE. The articles of the Franchisee shall reflect that the issuance and transfer of shares are restricted, and all share certificates shall bear the following legend, which shall be printed legibly and conspicuously on the back of each stock certificate:

       "The transfer of these shares is subject to the terms and conditions of a Franchise Agreement with THE SANDWICH TREE RESTAURANTS CORPORATION dated that date as set out in Rider 13. Reference is made to the said Franchise Agreement and to restrictive provisions of the Articles of this Corporation."

       The Franchisee acknowledges that the purpose of the aforesaid restrictions is to protect the Company's trademarks, service marks, trade secrets and operating procedures as well as the Company's general high reputation and image, and is for the mutual benefit of the Company, the Franchisee and other Franchisees and, notwithstanding any other terms of this Agreement, any failure by the Franchisee to comply with the terms of Clauses 10, 12, or 13, shall constitute a material breach of this Agreement and the Company shall have the right to terminate this Agreement upon seven (7) days written notice to the Franchisee.

24.   TRADEMARKS, TRADE NAMES, AND TRADE SECRETS. The Company represents, warrants and covenants that it has the right to grant to the Franchisee the rights granted herein. The Franchisee acknowledges the Company's rights (except for certain rights granted under existing and future licence agreements) to use the trademarks, trade names and trade secrets set forth herein, and represents, warrants and agrees that neither during the term of this Agreement, nor after the expiration or other termination hereof, shall the Franchisee directly or indirectly

contest or aid in contesting the validity or ownership of the Trademarks or take any action whatsoever in derogation of the Company's claimed rights therein, save and except any rights granted under a Registered User Agreement.

(a)   Nothing contained in this Agreement shall be construed to vest in the Franchisee any right, title or interest in or to THE SANDWICH TREE RESTAURANTS CORPORATION trademarks, the good will, now or hereafter associated therewith, or any right in the design of any restaurant premises, other than the rights and licences expressly granted herein, and subject to a Registered User Agreement. Any and all good will associated with THE SANDWICH TREE RESTAURANTS CORPORATION trademarks shall enure directly and exclusively to the benefit and is the property of the Company.

(b)   No advertising by the Franchisee or other use of the Company trademarks shall contain any statement or material which may, in the judgment of the Company, be in bad taste or inconsistent with the Company's public image. The Franchisee shall not use any advertising which has been disapproved by the Company for the reasons set forth in this Clause.

(c)   The Franchisee shall adopt and use the Company trademarks only in the manner expressly approved by the Company. The Franchisee shall advertise and promote the Restaurant only under the Company trademark and the name SANDWICH TREE without any accompanying words or symbols except as otherwise required by law and approved in writing by the Company.

(d)   Any information acquired by the Franchisee, either directly or indirectly, with respect to the operation of a SANDWICH TREE RESTAURANT, the business of the Company or any of the subject matters of this Agreement, is acknowledged to be classified information and strictly confidential, and no such information shall, at any time, be disclosed by the Franchisee to any other person, firm or corporation, except as to the minimum extent as in the opinion of the Company shall be absolutely essential to the carrying on of the said Restaurant business by the Franchisee.

(e)   The Franchisee acknowledges and agrees that the Company is the owner of all proprietary rights in and to the product formulas and restaurant systems and methods described in the Company's training manuals, guides, and materials, and that the product formulas and restaurant systems and methods in their entirety constitute trade secrets of the Company which are revealed to the Franchisee in confidence and that no right is given to or acquired by the Franchisee to disclose, duplicate, licence, sell or reveal any portion thereof to any person other than an employee of the Franchisee required by his work to be familiar with relevant portions thereof. The Franchisee hereby represents, warrants and agrees to keep and respect the confidence extended hereby. The Franchisee further acknowledges that the product formulas and other similar materials furnished to the Franchisee hereunder are and will remain the property of the Company, and must be returned to the Company immediately upon the termination of this Agreement.

(f)   The Franchisee shall have the right to use as a registered user the said Trademarks so long as this Agreement shall remain in force and the Company shall sign and execute the Registered User Agreement for the benefit of the Franchisee and the said Agreement to be registered with the Trademarks Office in Ottawa, Canada.

26.   NO AGENCY. No party shall represent or hold itself out as an agent, legal representative, partner, subsidiary, joint venturer or employee of any other party. No party shall have the right or power to, nor shall it bind or obligate any other party in any way, manner or thing whatsoever, nor represent that it has any right to do so. In all public records, and in its relationship with other persons, firms or corporations, on letterheads and business forms, the Franchisee shall indicate its independent ownership of the said business, and that it is only a Franchisee of the Company. The Franchisee agrees to

exhibit on the premises in a place designated by the Company, a notification that it is a Franchisee of the Company.

27.   DEFAULT BY FRANCHISEE. The occurrence of any of the following events shall constitute good cause for the Company, at its option, and without prejudice to any other rights or remedies provided for hereunder, or by law or equity, to terminate this Agreement.

(a)   If the Franchisee shall be adjudicated a bankrupt, becomes insolvent, or if a receiver (permanent or temporary) of its property or any part thereof is appointed by a court of competent authority; if it makes a general assignment for the benefit of creditors, or if a final judgment remains unsatisfied for thirty (30) days or longer after the period for appeal has expired or if execution is levied against the Franchisee's business or property, or suit to foreclose any lien or mortgage against the premises or equipment is instituted against the Franchisee and not contested within thirty (30) days; or if the Franchisee defaults in the performance of any term, condition or obligation in payment of any indebtedness to the Company, its suppliers, or others arising out of the purchase of supplies or purchase or lease of equipment for operation of its said restaurant, and if any such default is not cured within thirty (30) days after written notice by the Company to the Franchisee.

(b)   If the Franchisee defaults in the payment of royalties or advertising and sales promotion contributions due hereunder or fails to submit profit and loss statements or other financial statements of data, or reports on gross sales as provided herein, and if any such default is not cured within sixty (60) days after written notice by the Company to the Franchisee, or if the Franchisee knowingly makes any false statements in connection therewith.

(c)   If the Franchisee fails to maintain the standards as set forth in this Agreement, and as may be supplemented by the Manual, as to cleanliness, health and sanitation, and uniformity (including, without limitation, quality, and quantity of food products served), and if any such default is not cured within thirty (30) days after written notice by the Company to the Franchisee; or if the Franchisee repeatedly commits violations of such provisions.

(d)   If the Franchisee violates any law, ordinance, rule or regulation of a governmental agency in connection with its operation of the SANDWICH TREE RESTAURANT, and permits the same to remain unremedied thirty (30) days after notification thereof unless there is a bona fide dispute as to the violation or legality of such law, ordinance, rule or regulation, and the Franchisee promptly resorts to courts or forums of appropriate jurisdiction to contest such violation or legality.

(e)   If the Franchisee ceases to do business at the premises or defaults under any lease or sublease, or loses its right to the possession of the premises. Provided, however, that if the loss of possession is attributable to expropriation by any governmental authority, or if the premises are damaged or destroyed by a disaster of such nature that, in the opinion of the Company, the premises cannot be reasonably restored, then the Franchisee may relocate to other premises approved by the Company for the balance of the term hereof.

28.   DEFAULT BY THE COMPANY. The occurrence of any of the following events shall constitute good cause for the Franchisee, at its option, and without prejudice to any other rights, or remedies provided for hereunder or by law or equity, to terminate this Agreement:

(a)   If the Company shall be adjudicated a bankrupt, becomes insolvent, or if a receiver (permanent or temporary) of its property or any part thereof, is appointed by a court of competent authority; if it makes a general assignment for the benefit of creditors, or if a final judgment remains unsatisfied for thirty (30) days or longer after the period for appeal has expired or if execution is levied against the Company's business or property, and not contested within thirty (30) days.

(b)   If the premises are leased by the Franchisee from the Company, and the Company defaults under that Lease or loses its rights to possession of the premises. Provided, however, that if the loss of possession is attributable to expropriation by any governmental authority, or if the premises are damaged or destroyed by a disaster of such nature that, in the opinion of the Company, the premises cannot be reasonably restored, then the Franchisee, may, at its discretion, relocate to other premises approved by the Company for the balance of the term hereof.

29.   <u>EFFECT OF TERMINATION BY FRANCHISEE</u>. Upon termination of this Agreement by lapse of time upon occasion of default by either the Franchisee or the Company, the Franchisee's right to use in any manner the service marks or any other mark registered by the Company or insignia or slogan used in connection therewith, or any confusingly similar trade-mark, service mark, trade name or insignia, shall terminate forthwith, the Franchisee shall not thereafter directly or indirectly identify itself in any manner as a Franchisee, or publicly identify itself as a former Franchisee or use any of the Company's trade secrets, signs, symbols, devices, recipes, formulas, food mixes or other materials constituting part of the system. The Franchisee grants to the Company the option to purchase within thirty (30) days of notice by the Franchisee all paper goods, containers, signs, menus and any and all insignia bearing the Company's trade name or marks thereon at the lower of cost or fair market value at the time of termination.

(a)   If the premises are leased from the Company and termination arises out of a default in performance of any term of this Agreement, by the Franchisee, the Company may offer to purchase within thirty (30) days of termination the Franchisee's comestibles at its acquisition price, and to purchase its restaurant equipment at its depreciated value. Depreciated value shall be the lesser of market value or Franchisee's cost less depreciation on a straight-line basis of ten (10%) per cent per year.

(b)   If the premises are not leased from the Company, upon termination of this Agreement by lapse of time or default by either the Franchisee or the Company, the Franchisee shall immediately make such removals or changes in signs and colours of buildings and structures as the Company shall reasonably request so to distinguish effectively the premises from their former appearance and from any other SANDWICH TREE RESTAURANT. If the Franchisee shall fail to make such changes forthwith, then the Company may enter upon the Franchisee's premises and make such changes at the Franchisee's expense.

(c)   In the event of termination arising out of any default by the Franchisee, the extent of all damage which the Company has suffered by virtue of, and as direct consequence, such default shall be and remain a lien in favour of the Company against any and all of the personal property, machinery, fixtures and equipment owned by the Franchisee at the time of such default.

30.   <u>EFFECT OF TERMINATION BY COMPANY</u>. In the event of termination of this Agreement by the Company:

(a)   If the premises are leased by the Company and termination of the Lease arises out of a default in the performance of the term of the Lease by the Company, then the Franchisee shall no longer be bound by its lease or sublease with the Company, and the Franchisee may, at its discretion, negotiate directly with the Lessor of the Company or its affiliates regarding the leasing of the premises.

(b)   If any of the restaurant equipment utilized by the Franchisee is leased from the Company, and termination arises out of a default in performance of the terms of this Agreement by the Company, the Franchisee may offer to purchase within thirty (30) days of termination, that Company's equipment at its depreciated value. Depreciated value shall be the lesser of market value or Company's costs less depreciation on a straight-line basis of ten (10%) per cent per year.

(c)   If termination arises out of a default in the performance of the terms of this Agreement by the Company, the Franchisee shall not be responsible for payment of any royalties or advertising and sales promotion contributions as determined pursuant to this Agreement.

(d)   In the event of termination for any default of the Company, the extent of all damage which the Franchisee has suffered by virtue of, and as a direct consequence, such default, shall be and remain a lien in favour of the Franchisee against any and all of the personal property, machinery, fixtures, and equipment owned by the Company on the premises at the time of such default.

31.   ARBITRATION. If this Agreement shall be terminated by the Company, and the Franchisee shall dispute the Company's right of termination, or the reasonableness thereof, the parties shall submit such dispute to a single arbitrator to be agreed upon by the Company, and the Franchisee, and any arbitration hereunder shall be made pursuant to the provisions of the Arbitration Act, Revised Statutes of British Columbia, Chapter 18.

32.   INTERPRETATION. The preamble recitals are incorporated in and made a part of this Agreement. Titles of clauses and paragraphs are used for convenience only, and are not a part of the text. All terms used in any one number or gender shall be construed to include any other number or gender as the context may require.

33.   ENTIRE AGREEMENT. This Agreement constitutes the entire Agreement of the parties and supercedes all prior negotiations, agreements, commitments, representations, and undertakings of the parties with respect to the subject matter hereof, and the Franchisee agrees that the Company has made no representations inducing execution of this Agreement which are not included herein.

34.   NON-WAIVER. The failure of any party to exercise any right, power or option given to it hereunder, shall not constitute a waiver of the terms and conditons of this Agreement with respect to any other or subsequent breach thereof, nor a waiver by any party of its rights at any time thereafter to require exact and strict compliance with all the terms hereof. The rights or remedies hereunder are cumulative to any other rights or remedies which may be granted by law.

35.   GOVERNING LAW. This Agreement shall become valid when executed and accepted by the Company at the City of Vancouver, in the Province of British Columbia, and it shall be governed and construed under and in accordance with the laws of the Province of British Columbia. Anything herein to the contrary notwithstanding, the Franchisee and the Company shall conduct their business in a lawful manner; and they will faithfully comply with all applicable laws or regulations of the Province, City or other political subdivisions in which they conduct their said business.

36.   SEVERABILITY. If any provisions of this Agreement are held invalid by arbitration or court decree, such finding shall not invalidate the remainder of this Agreement.

37.   NOTICES. All notices or other communications required or permitted to be given hereunder shall be in writing, and may be given by mailing in an envelope or wrapper, postage prepaid, addressed to the respective parties as set out in Rider 14, or such other address as any party may indicate to the other parties hereto in writing. Any notice may be sent by registered mail, and if so mailed, from any governmental post office in Vancouver, British Columbia, shall be

deemed to have been received by the party to whom it is addressed, if delivered, when delivered, and if so mailed, on the second business day active, exclusive of Saturday, Sunday and Statutory holidays, after the time of registration and posting thereof.

38.   EMPLOYEES. The Company shall have no control over employees of the Franchisee, including the terms and conditions of their employment.

39.   COMPETITION WITH THE COMPANY. The Franchisee agrees that during the term of this Agreement, and any renewal thereof, it shall not engage in any restaurant or prepared food business which is the same or similar to the Company's business. The Franchisee further agrees that, for a period of eighteen (18) months after termination of this Agreement, it will not engage in any business the same or similar to the Company's business within that area set out in Rider 15 from the premises without the prior written consent of the Company. In applying for the Company's consent, the Franchisee has the burden of establishing that any such activity by it will not involve the use of benefits provide hereby or constitute unfair competition with the Company or other Franchisees of the Company.

40.   INTERFERENCE WITH EMPLOYMENT RELATIONS OF OTHERS. The Franchisee shall not attempt to attain an unfair advantage over the Company or other Franchisees of the Company by soliciting for employment any person who is, at the time of such solicitation, employed by the Company or by other Franchisees of the Company, nor shall the Franchisee directly or indirectly induce any such person to leave his or her employment as aforesaid.

41.   LIABILITY OF GUARANTOR. In consideration of the sum of ONE ($1.00) DOLLAR now paid by the Company to the Guarantor, and other valuable consideration, (the receipt whereof is hereby acknowledged), the Guarantor hereby covenants with the Company that the Franchisee shall duly perform and observe each and every covenant, proviso, condition and agreement in this Agreement on the part of the Franchisee to be performed and observed, and that if any default be made by the Franchisee, the Guarantor shall, forthwith pay to the Franchisee, on demand, such sum in respect of which such default shall have occurred, and all damages that may arise in direct consequence of the non-observance, and non-performance of any of the said covenants, provisos, conditions and agreements. The Guarantor covenants with the Company that the Guarantor is jointly and severally bound with the Franchisee for the fulfillment of all obligations of the Franchisee under this Agreement. In the enforcement of its rights hereunder, the Company may proceed against the Guarantor as if the Guarantor were named the Franchisee hereunder, and the Guarantor hereby waives any right to require the Company to proceed against the Franchisee or to proceed against or to exhaust any security held by the Company, or to pursue any other remedy whatsoever which may be available to the Company before proceeding against the Guarantor.

42.   MODIFICATION. This Agreement may only be modified or amended by written agreement.

43.   EXECUTION. This Agreement is executed in triplicate originals, any one of which may be introduced into evidence as conclusive proof of the context thereof. The Agreement shall be binding upon the parties, their heirs, executors, administrators, successors and assigns.

SAMPLE FRANCHISE CONTRACT — Continued

IN WITNESS WHEREOF, the parties have executed this Agreement as of the date and year first above written.

THE CORPORATE SEAL of THE SANDWICH)
TREE RESTAURANTS CORPORATION was   )
hereunto affixed in the presence   )
of:)
)
)
_____,)
)
                      _____)
       Authorized signatory   )

THE CORPORATE SEAL of   )
              was hereunto affixed)
in the presence of:)
)
)
_____)
)
                      _____)
       Authorized signatory   )

SIGNED, SEALED AND DELIVERED by   )
the Guarantor in the presence of:)
)
)
Name:_____   )
)
Address:_____   )
)
Occupation:_____   )

<u>FRANCHISE AGREEMENT</u>

BETWEEN:

THE SANDWICH TREE RESTAURANT CORPORATION

and

<u>RIDERS</u>

Rider No.	Page No.	Clause No.	Subject	
1	2	1	Franchise Payment Canadian	$_____
2	5	4	Location	
3	5	5	Area _____ Miles of the premises	
4	5	6	Term	_____
5	7	9	Royalties	_____ %
6	7	10	Advertising and Sales Promotion	_____ %
7	8	12	Accounting Fee	$_____
8	14	16	Insurance on Fixtures and Tenant's Improvement	$_____
9	14	16	Tenant's fire Legal Liability	$_____
10	14	16	Replacement value of stock	$_____
11	15	19	Option to Renew	_____ years
12	17	20	Shareholders	_____
13	18	23	Articles of Franchisee	_____
14	29	37	Notices to The Company: 120-535 West 10th Avenue Vancouver, B. C. The Franchisee: The Guarantor:	
15	30	39	Competition with the Company _____ Miles	

SELF-COUNSEL SERIES

CANADIAN

ORDER FORM

SELF-COUNSEL SERIES

05/87

NATIONAL TITLES:

_____ Abbreviations & Acronyms	5.95
_____ Aids to Independence	11.95
_____ Asking Questions	7.95
_____ Assertiveness for Managers	8.95
_____ Basic Accounting	5.95
_____ Be a Better Manager	8.95
_____ Best Ways to Make Money	5.95
_____ Better Book for Getting Hired	9.95
_____ Between the Sexes	8.95
_____ Business Guide to Effective Speaking	6.95
_____ Business Guide to Telephone Systems	7.95
_____ Business Writing Workbook	9.95
_____ Buying (and Selling) a Small Business	6.95
_____ Civil Rights	8.95
_____ Collection Techniques for the Small Business	4.95
_____ Complete Guide to Home Contracting	19.95
_____ Conquering Compulsive Eating	5.95
_____ Credit, Debt, and Bankruptcy	7.95
_____ Criminal Procedure in Canada	14.95
_____ Design Your Own Logo	9.95
_____ Drinking and Driving	4.50
_____ Editing Your Newsletter	14.95
_____ Entrepreneur's Self-Assessment Guide	9.95
_____ Family Ties That Bind	7.95
_____ Federal Incorporation and Business Guide	14.95
_____ Financial Control for the Small Business	6.95
_____ Financial Freedom on $5 a Day	7.95
_____ For Sale By Owner	6.95
_____ Forming and Managing a Non-Profit Organization in Canada	12.95
_____ Franchising in Canada	6.50
_____ Fundraising	5.50
_____ Getting Elected	8.95
_____ Getting Sales	14.95
_____ Getting Started	10.95
_____ How to Advertise	7.95
_____ How You Too Can Make a Million . . . in the Mail Order Business	9.95
_____ Immigrating to Canada	14.95
_____ Immigrating to U.S.A.	14.95
_____ Insuring Business Risks	3.50
_____ Keyboarding for Kids	7.95
_____ Landlording in Canada	12.95
_____ Learn to Type Fast	9.95
_____ Managing Your Office Records & Files	14.95
_____ Managing Stress	7.95
_____ Marketing Your Service	12.95
_____ Media Law Handbook	6.50
_____ Medical Law Handbook	6.95
_____ Mike Grenby's Tax Tips	6.95
_____ Mortgages & Foreclosure	7.95
_____ Musician's Handbook	7.95
_____ A Nanny For Your Child	7.95
_____ Newcomer's Guide to the U.S.A.	12.95
_____ Parent's Guide to Day Care	5.95
_____ Patent Your Own Invention	21.95
_____ Photography & The Law	7.95
_____ Practical Guide to Financial Management	6.95
_____ Radio Documentary Handbook	8.95
_____ Ready-to-Use Business Forms	9.95
_____ Retirement Guide for Canadians	9.95
_____ Small Business Guide to Employee Selection	6.95
_____ Start and Run a Profitable Beauty Salon	14.95
_____ Start and Run a Profitable Consulting Business	12.95
_____ Start and Run a Profitable Craft Business	10.95
_____ Start and Run a Profitable Home Typing Business	9.95
_____ Start and Run a Profitable Restaurant	10.95
_____ Start and Run a Profitable Retail Business	11.95
_____ Start and Run a Profitable Video Store	10.95
_____ Starting a Successful Business in Canada	12.95
_____ Step-Parent Adoptions	12.95
_____ Taking Care	7.95
_____ Tax Law Handbook	12.95
_____ Tax Shelters	7.95
_____ Trusts and Trust Companies	3.95

_____ Upper Left-Hand Corner	10.95
_____ Using the Access to Information Act	5.95
_____ Word Processing	8.95
_____ Working Couples	5.50
_____ Write Right!	5.50

PROVINCIAL TITLES:

Divorce Guide
☐ B.C. 9.95 ☐ Alberta 9.95 ☐ Ontario 12.95
☐ Manitoba 11.95 ☐ Saskatchewan

Employer/Employee Rights
☐ B.C. 6.95 ☐ Alberta 6.95 ☐ Ontario 6.95

Fight That Ticket
☐ B.C. 5.95

Incorporation Guide
☐ B.C. 14.95 ☐ Alberta 14.95 ☐ Ontario 14.95
☐ Manitoba/Saskatchewan 12.95

Landlord/Tenant Rights
☐ B.C. 7.95 ☐ Alberta 6.95 ☐ Ontario 7.95

Marriage & Family Law
☐ B.C. 7.95 ☐ Alberta 8.95 ☐ Ontario 7.95

Probate Guide
☐ B.C. 12.95 ☐ Alberta 9.95 ☐ Ontario 11.95

Real Estate Guide
☐ B.C. 7.95 ☐ Alberta 7.95 ☐ Ontario 7.95

Small Claims Court Guide
☐ B.C. 7.95 ☐ Alberta 7.50 ☐ Ontario 7.50

Wills
☐ B.C. 6.50 ☐ Alberta 5.95 ☐ Ontario 5.95

Wills/Probate Procedure
☐ Manitoba/Saskatchewan 5.95

PACKAGED FORMS:

Divorce Forms
☐ B.C. 9.95 ☐ Alberta 10.95 ☐ Ontario 14.95
☐ Manitoba 10.95 ☐ Saskatchewan 12.95

Incorporation
☐ B.C. 12.95 ☐ Alberta 14.95 ☐ Ontario 14.95
☐ Manitoba 14.95 ☐ Saskatchewan 14.95 ☐ Federal 7.95

Minute Books 17.95

Probate
☐ B.C. Administration 14.95 ☐ B.C. Probate 14.95 ☐ Alberta 14.95
☐ Ontario 15.50

☐ Rental Form Kit (B.C., Alberta, Ontario, Saskatchewan)	5.95
☐ Have You Made Your Will?	5.95
☐ If You Love Me Put It In Writing Contract Kit	14.95
☐ If You Leave Me Put It In Writing B.C. Separation Agreement Kit	14.95

NOTE: All prices are subject to change without notice.

Books are available in book and department stores, or use the order form below.

Please enclose cheque or money order (plus sales tax where applicable) or give us your MasterCard or Visa number (please include validation and expiry date).

(PLEASE PRINT)

Name _____

Address _____

City _____ Province _____ Postal Code _____

☐ Visa/☐ MasterCard Number _____

Validation Date _____ Expiry Date _____

If order is under $20.00, add $1.00 for postage and handling.

Please send orders to:

INTERNATIONAL SELF-COUNSEL PRESS LTD.   ☐ Check here for free catalogue.
1481 Charlotte Road
North Vancouver, British Columbia
V7J 1H1

TITLES AVAILABLE
FROM
SELF-COUNSEL PRESS

MEDIA LAW HANDBOOK
Every person in the news industry and every book author or publisher will find this book invaluable. The structure of the Canadian news industry is given as a background to a concise discussion of CRTC regulations, copyright laws, reporting on criminal trials, and much more.

THE CONSUMER BOOK
Consumers' rights under the various consumer protection acts and federal legislation are carefully explained and practical tips are provided on how "victims" can protect themselves.

DIVORCE GUIDE
Our *Divorce Guide* is the original do-it-yourself aid. It is the most complete and up-to-date publication available on how to obtain an uncontested divorce.

IMMIGRATING TO CANADA
This guide explains how the Canadian immigration system works and how to become a legal immigrant. Examples of application forms are included.

IMMIGRATING TO THE U.S.A.
Written by a Seattle lawyer specializing in immigration law, this is a complete guide to how to immigrate to the U.S. It is useful for the prospective immigrant and for relatives in the U.S. who are trying to help.

LANDLORD/TENANT RIGHTS
This book provides both the landlord and the tenant with a working knowledge of the law in the landlord/tenant relationship. Areas covered include tenancy agreements, rent increases, security deposits, repairs, right to privacy, and evictions.

MARRIAGE & FAMILY LAW
Of particular interest to women, this book deals with all aspects of the marriage and family institution and explains how to use the law to protect your rights.

A PARENTS' GUIDE TO DAY CARE
This comprehensive consumer's guide to child care alternatives shows parents how to inform themselves about the choices and how to make day care a positive experience.

PROBATE GUIDE
This book shows, in non-technical language, how to apply for and obtain letters probate or administration and transfer the assets to the beneficiaries, without the help or cost of a lawyer.

REAL ESTATE BUYING/SELLING GUIDE
The author includes an excellent introduction to the general area of real estate as well as a discussion of commercial mortgages, government loans and grants, and sale and purchase of real estate.

RESORT CONDOS AND TIMESHARING
High pressure sales tactics and glittery come-ons have caused many unwary people to get in over their heads when purchasing a vacation condominium or timeshare. This book explains the difference between the good and bad ones and can save a buyer thousands of dollars.

RETIREMENT GUIDE
For those who are unprepared, retirement is both a shock and a disappointment. This guide gives counsel on how to prepare for a healthy, happy, and financially secure retirement.

SMALL CLAIMS COURT GUIDE
This book is a complete manual to proceeding with or defending an action in small claims court. It includes samples of forms and a step-by-step explanation of the procedure involved in an action.

WILLS
This book explains the whys and hows of writing a will and indicates the complications that arise in relation to wills and estate planning.

WORKING COUPLES

Being a working couple doesn't have to mean having constant conflict in your life. This practical guide takes a straight-forward approach to the issues involved when both people in a relationship are working outside the home.

BETTER BOOK FOR GETTING HIRED

The focus of this book is on the importance of the resume. You may be short changing yourself by not giving the prospective employer an accurate picture of your talents. If you feel this is the case, then this book is for you.

CREDIT, DEBT, AND BANKRUPTCY

This handbook is for persons who buy on credit, which includes just about all of us. Beginning with a general overview of the Canadian credit situation, it then turns to discussing each credit institution in detail. It suggests how to handle debt harassment, debt pooling, and bankruptcy.

CIVIL RIGHTS

An excellent guide to Canadian civil rights, this book covers many offences punishable under summary conviction as well as the more serious criminal offences. It has been updated to explain the effect of the new Charter of Rights and Freedoms.

CRIMINAL PROCEDURE IN CANADA

For the lawyer, police officer, or anyone who has more than the occasional involvement with the courts, this book is an invaluable ready reference guide. It covers all areas of the law from the time of arrest through to convictions or releases and appeals.

FOR SALE BY OWNER

If you want to save thousands of dollars on real estate commissions when you sell your house, this book will tell you the proven techniques you need to know in order to succeed.

MORTGAGES AND FORECLOSURE

This book cuts through the legal jargon of a home mortgage contract and explains what should and shouldn't concern the buyer. It describes different types of mortgages available in today's market and how to use a mortgage as an investment.

MANAGING YOUR OFFICE RECORDS AND FILES

This book outlines a step-by-step methodology for offices and organizations of any size to take charge of files and assure access to information.

BUSINESS TITLES

ASSERTIVENESS FOR MANAGERS

Valuable advice for anyone in a supervisory position is given on effective skills for managing people. Exercises are included.

ADVERTISING FOR THE SMALL BUSINESS

Tells you from start to finish how to advertise effectively even if you have never done it before. It explains the jargon and illustrates the basic principles of every medium of advertising.

BASIC ACCOUNTING FOR THE SMALL BUSINESS

Discusses day-to-day accounting problems encountered in running a small business. Instructions for preliminary bookkeeping and organizing financial matters are given.

BUSINESS GUIDE TO TELEPHONE SYSTEMS

Difficult choices are made easy in this readable guide to the communications technology. This book guides the business person through the maze of regulations, basic systems, systems management, and needs assessment.

BUYING (AND SELLING) A SMALL BUSINESS

Buying a business is often the easiest way to become an entrepreneur. This book shows how to carefully investigate the potential profitability of a business, how to assess the asking price, and how to be sure you get what you paid for.

COLLECTION TECHNIQUES
FOR THE SMALL BUSINESS

When polite reminders about overdue accounts don't bring anything but polite excuses, you don't have to give up. You can use the same successful techniques that the professionals use to collect money.

FUNDRAISING FOR NON-PROFIT GROUPS
Raising money is the most essential and also the most difficult task for any organization. This book explains how to do it, from making up the budget to approaching corporation presidents and other possible funders.

GETTING SALES
Designed to serve sales people, independent retailers, small and large manufacturers, service businesses and consultants, this book provides step-by-step instructions for finding more customers and increasing sales.

GETTING STARTED
If you want to go into business for yourself, either part-time or full-time, you will need to know every sales and marketing tip there is. *Getting Started* offers tips to fight inflation, increase sales, use effective advertising, and increase the success of your business.

LEARN TO TYPE FAST
This book provides a unique method of learning how to type. This new system, which you can learn in five hours, teaches you the keys in relation to your fingers, rather than the keyboard.

STARTING A SUCCESSFUL BUSINESS
Information regarding tax laws, purchasing an existing business, and the entire field of successful business operation is authoritatively discussed and well-explained.

WORD PROCESSING HANDBOOK
This book describes the kinds of machines available and evaluates them in terms of individual businesses and their needs. It shows how to shop for the word processor you need.

WRITE RIGHT!
The author, a professional writer and editor, shows how to write effectively with little effort. She explains when to use certain words and phrases, where the commas go, and how to say what you really mean.

EDITING YOUR NEWSLETTER
This book is for anyone who edits a regular newsletter. It discusses how to establish the goals of your newsletter, how to distribute it, how to produce a quality item with a limited budget, and how to gather news regularly.

EMPLOYEE/EMPLOYER GUIDE
Offers a clear explanation of labor law, including labor standards regarding age of employment, wages, hours of work, rest periods, maternity leave, and much more.

EXPORTING
Details are given about what to look for in developing export markets, what pitfalls to beware of, how to deal with foreign businesses, and how to do the tons of necessary paperwork in order to export.

IMPORTING
There are thousands of regulations and dozens of forms involved in importing, and this comprehensive guide explains what they're all about.

INCORPORATION GUIDE
The practice and theory of establishing a private limited company, along with the principles of limited liability are outlined and clarified. Step-by-step instructions for incorporating your company are included.

FINANCIAL CONTROL FOR THE SMALL BUSINESS
In easy-to-understand language, this book takes you through the "after the basics" accounting procedure for the small business, and shows how your accounts affect your business, and how you can increase sales and success by gaining control of your books.

FRANCHISING
Buying a franchise can be a good, lower-risk way to go into business for yourself, but it is not an instant road to success. Here is an explanation of royalty terms, franchise sites, and unethical pyramid schemes. Included is a questionnaire to help the buyer identify suitable franchises and practical advice for finding a good investment.